LEADING

Change

in Your School

How to Conquer Myths, Build
Commitment, and Get Results

ASCD MEMBER BOOK

Many ASCD members received this book as a member benefit upon its initial release.

Learn more at: **www.ascd.org/memberbooks**

ASCD cares about Planet Earth.
This book has been printed on environmentally friendly paper.

DOUGLAS B. REEVES

LEADING
Change
IN YOUR
School

How to Conquer Myths, Build
Commitment, and Get Results

ASCD
Alexandria, Virginia USA

Association for Supervision and Curriculum Development
1703 N. Beauregard St. • Alexandria, VA 22311-1714 USA
Phone: 800-933-2723 or 703-578-9600 • Fax: 703-575-5400
Web site: www.ascd.org • E-mail: member@ascd.org
Author guidelines: www.ascd.org/write

Gene R. Carter, *Executive Director*; Nancy Modrak, *Publisher*; Julie Houtz, *Director of Book Editing &
Production*; Miriam Goldstein, *Project Manager*; Greer Wymond, *Senior Graphic Designer*; Mike Kalyan,
Production Manager; Keith Demmons, *Typesetter*; Carmen Yuhas, *Production Specialist*

Printed in the United States of America. Cover art copyright © 2009 by ASCD. ASCD publications present a variety of viewpoints. The views expressed or implied in this book should not be interpreted as official
positions of the Association.

All Web links in this book are correct as of the publication date below but may have become inactive or
otherwise modified since that time. If you notice a deactivated or changed link, please e-mail books@ascd.
org with the words "Link Update" in the subject line. In your message, please specify the Web link, the
book title, and the page number on which the link appears.

ASCD Member Book, No. FY09-6 (Apr. 2009, PS). ASCD Member Books mail to Premium (P) and Select
(S) members on this schedule: Jan., PS; Feb., P; Apr., PS; May, P; July, PS; Aug., P; Sept., PS; Nov., PS; Dec.,
P. Select membership was formerly known as Comprehensive membership.

PAPERBACK ISBN: 978-1-4166-0808-0   ASCD product #109019

Also available as an e-book through ebrary, netLibrary, and many online booksellers (see Books in Print for
the ISBNs).

Quantity discounts for the paperback edition only: 10–49 copies, 10%; 50+ copies, 15%; for 1,000 or more
copies, call 800-933-2723, ext. 5634, or 703-575-5634. For desk copies: member@ascd.org.

Library of Congress Cataloging-in-Publication Data
Reeves, Douglas B., 1953-
  Leading change in your school : how to conquer myths, build commitment, and get results / Douglas B.
Reeves.
      p. cm.
  Includes bibliographical references and index.
  ISBN 978-1-4166-0808-0 (pbk. : alk. paper) 1. School management and organization–United States.
2. Educational change–United States. 3. Educational leadership–United States. 4. School improvement
programs–United States. I. Title.

  LB2805.R416 2009
  371.200973–dc22

                          2008053691

18 17 16 15 14 13 12 11 10 09   1 2 3 4 5 6 7 8 9 10 11 12

For Cathy Shulkin

Leading Change in Your School

How to Conquer Myths, Build Commitment, and Get Results

Acknowledgments

The debts of an author always outstrip the power of acknowledgments. I offer these public accolades as only the beginning of the appreciation that these wonderful colleagues deserve. By my rough calculation, Cathy Shulkin has edited more than a million words from my pen during the last eight years, and approximately 999,999 of those words required revision. When she needed a break from editing this manuscript, she presided over a wedding and led major projects for The Leadership and Learning Center. She makes my life easier in precisely the proportion to which I make hers more difficult. Miriam Goldstein engaged in another partnership with ASCD and me, and her insightful suggestions and critical eye were essential contributions to this book. I am particularly indebted to Marge Scherer, Editor in Chief of the world's leading education journal, *Educational Leadership*, for her thought leadership in education, for encouraging my work in monthly columns, and for permitting me to use that material in this book. Deborah Perkins-Gough, Senior Editor of *Educational Leadership*, regularly challenges me to provide better evidence and examples, focus my ideas, and consider that busy school leaders have a few other priorities on their plate than reading 3,000 words when 750 will do very nicely.

And I thank the following people at ASCD for their ongoing support: Gene Carter, Executive Director; Nancy Modrak, Publisher; and Scott Willis, Director of Book Acquisitions and Development.

My work on change leadership has been profoundly influenced by many writers and practitioners, but a few stand out as people willing to engage me in dialogue and challenge my thinking. Therefore, I am particularly indebted to Larry Ainsworth, Elle Allison, Roland Barth, Melinda Boone, Lucy Calkins, Linda Darling-Hammond, Rebecca DuFour, Richard DuFour, Richard Elmore, Ron Ferguson, Michael Fullan, Howard Gardner, Bill Habermehl, Andy Hargreaves, Jeff Howard, Timothy Jenney, Thom Lockamy, Robert Marzano, Brian McNulty, Ken O'Connor, Mia Pollock, Richard Rothstein, Mike Schmoker, Terry Thompson, Mike Wasta, Tim Waters, Margaret Wheatley, Grant Wiggins, and Chris Wright. My colleagues at The Leadership and Learning Center have been the support structure that has allowed me to pursue my passions for leadership, teaching, learning, and research. They now number 80 and growing, and they know who they are. I am also grateful to The Leadership and Learning Center and Margaret Lush, its president, for permission to use material on change readiness in Chapters 2 and 3.

The most important acknowledgment by teachers is of our students, and while I will not call them by name, I know that on the Friday morning after I write this, I will see 25 teenagers who are not terribly interested in my theories and research. These students are preoccupied and anxious not only for themselves but also for their families. They are positive that their peers and many in their community do not value their academic performance. Certainly they know that their bow-tied teacher is a stark raving lunatic for thinking that kids who are hearing-impaired, who do not speak English well, who have difficulty reading and writing, or who are angry and disengaged will be, before year's end, polished, engaging, and competitive speakers and writers.

The life of a teacher is to elevate hope and confidence above cynicism and despair, if only by the slightest measure. My wish for the readers of this volume is not that they find a magic formula or misplace their confidence in another false solution, but that their hope and confidence match those of the students we serve.

Introduction

Here is a simple recipe for leading change. First, pour a truckload of evidence into an ungreased container. Stir in a crock full of inspirational rhetoric. Add two heaping portions of administrative imperatives. Finally, dump into the mix precisely one ton of fear. Bring to a boil.

If this recipe were effective, then change leadership would not be the single greatest challenge for organizations around the world—not only in education, but also in business, government, professional practices, and nonprofit organizations. Deutschman (2007) demonstrates that the typical combination of evidence, authority, and fear is insufficient to lead the vast majority of people to make decisions that will save their own lives, gain years with their loved ones, and avoid painful and debilitating illness and eventual death. The fear of pain and death is not, for many people, greater than their unwillingness to change. In the business world, the results of failed change efforts have "been appalling, with wasted resources and burned-out, scared, or frustrated employees" (Kotter, 2006, p. 4). Despite the potential cataclysmic effects of global warming, the current wave of environmentalism is best represented by rock stars addressing conferences on climate change, transported to the affair by private jet and a Hummer limousine. It is little wonder that change in educational systems is elusive. Vander Ark (Wagner, Kegan, Lahey, & Lemons, 2006) summarized the challenges well when he noted, "This work is hard—it's complicated, technical, personal, and political" (p. xi).

In my attempts to advise almost 200,000 readers of *Educational Leadership* every month about leading change, I have had the unexpected pleasure of an e-mail inbox overflowing with helpful ripostes, a sample of which include the following:

- "I've always been a collaborative leader, and I know that we have to get buy-in from all the stakeholders before we can start a successful change effort. Therefore, until you can explain to me how to get buy-in from everyone, I'm afraid that change will have to wait."

- "Of course I want to change—it's just that everyone else is resisting it."

- "I believe you, Doug—really. It's just that no one else in my school does. So I'm afraid that change is quite impossible right now."

These correspondents are my colleagues, my friends, my readers. Writers like me wouldn't be worth much without them. On the other hand, writers like me aren't worth much more than another gust of hot air unless our readers actually do something. Unless words are transformed into action, then we are the proverbial clanging gong, generating lots of noise but little meaning. The result of paralysis in the face of change is toxic and counterproductive. As Schmoker (2006) concludes, "our typical attempts to reform our schools not only fail but will have a corrupting effect as we engage in the pretense of instructional improvement" (p. 30).

The overwhelming challenges of change inevitably lead to cynicism. When employees are treated as the detritus of change efforts rather than the keys to effective change implementation, then organizations cannot be surprised that firms such as Despair, Inc. thrive. Despair markets what it calls "demotivators," such as a poster with a picture of a salmon leaping into the mouth of a hungry bear, along with the caption "The journey of a thousand miles sometimes ends very, very badly." The poster with the title "Change" has a vivid picture of a tornado and the caption "When the winds of change blow hard enough, the most trivial of things can turn into deadly projectiles." My favorite is the one titled "Despair," with the caption "It's always darkest just before it goes pitch black."

It doesn't have to be this way. Fullan (2008) tells us encouragingly that we can create FOEs—Firms of Endearment—by engaging our colleagues rather than manipulating them. In more than two-and-a-half million miles of travel to schools in every part of the world, I have found a growing number of change leaders. These are the people who not only implement change successfully, but also appear to thrive on it. Their colleagues are no more insightful, desperate, or well informed than average. Their circumstances are neither more dire nor more comfortable, so change is executed neither at the edge of a sword nor in the security of a riskless environment. Rather, these change leaders share a common commitment to the notion that ideas are more important than personalities. They challenge the popular leadership literature that elevates charisma over character, machismo over modesty.

The change leaders described in this book are veterans and novices, women and men; they represent a broad spectrum of cultures and backgrounds. They are introverts and extroverts, teachers and administrators, exceptional and ordinary. You will not find "Leadership by Attila the Hun" in the following pages any more than you will find the elusive attributes of saints. You will find, I hope, people like you, sharing similar challenges but perhaps with different results. Their stories are completely authentic. Unlike what frequently passes for "research" that is veiled in anonymity and rarely, if ever, verifiable, you will read about real people and real schools, with names and locations clearly identified.

We begin with a consideration of the conditions for change. Educational leaders are expert in announcing change, scattering the seeds of promising ideas. But they are considerably less adept at moving aside the initiatives of the previous year so that the seeds of the new announcement have the slightest opportunity to take root. Hence the injunction that we must "pull the weeds" before we "plant new flowers." You will also find Change Readiness Assessments for individuals and organizations, tools that could be useful to complete before you embark on the next change initiative. Culture is deeply ingrained in educational institutions, and so we closely examine what it takes to change school culture. The first part of the book closes with a consideration of myths related to change and leadership.

The second part of the book considers planning for change, which involves a combination of people and process, with the former beating the latter by a good distance. It isn't that strategic planning, as it is frequently practiced, is worthless. It can actually be much worse than that, with counterproductive results that are sustained far longer than the changes the strategists purported to plan. Fortunately, there are effective planning models that replace piles of three-ring binders with highly focused goals and action plans. Individual and small-group actions, which formulate the essence of successful change, can be nurtured and sustained with effective coaching. However, just as "strategic planning" has frequently been anything but strategic, so also "coaching" represents a range of meanings, from pseudotherapy to a catalyst for performance that transforms individuals and organizations.

Third, we consider the essentials of change implementation, using real examples of elementary and secondary schools that have moved change initiatives from rhetoric to reality. Although many change initiatives focus on the basics of literacy and math, the evidence from this part of the book reminds us that successful schools, including those with enormous demographic challenges, see the arts not as a frill but as an integral part of the intellectual and academic development of their students. We also confront the significant difference between what change leaders say and what they do. This chasm is the result not of malice or ineptitude, but rather of a lack of descriptive rigor. When, for example, we hear terms such as "instructional leadership," the difference between vapid slogans and meaningful implementation comes down to the details of daily conversations and decisions by leaders in classrooms and schools.

In the fourth part of the book we consider the issue of sustaining change. Hargreaves and Fink (2006) remind us that international lessons, from Scandinavia to Zambia, shed some light on the essential nature that culture plays in sustaining meaningful change. Sustainability has less to do with five-year plans redolent of Stalin and more to do with the perspective that those responsible for change have outside of themselves. Here we find the missing ingredient in the recipe. Evidence is, of course, important. Administrative clarity is essential. Fear can be not only a natural human reaction to the evidence but also a powerful and even an appropriate element of the change equation. But if we have learned anything over the past several decades of research in change leadership, it is that evidence, commands, and fears are insufficient to create change at either the individual or the organizational level. Sustainable change requires a reorientation of priorities and values so that the comfort and convenience of the individual is no longer the measure by which the legitimacy of change is considered. Rather, we respond to a vision of change that is so compelling and whose benefits for others are so overwhelming that we see students and colleagues not as cogs in the machine but as stars in a galaxy that outshines our fears and dwarfs our apprehensions. At the same time—and this is the key to change leadership—we know that each star in the firmament holds an essential place, and without it, a constellation would be diminished. Thus the paradox of change leadership is the elevation of a vision far greater than the individual and, at the same time, the elevation of the individual to a place that is unique, powerful, and essential. You are about to meet leaders who have done precisely that.

If you would like to continue the dialogue and share your own stories of successful change leadership, log on to www.Change Leaders.info, a noncommercial Web site devoted exclusively to sharing research, case studies, and ideas about successful change leadership.

PART 1

Creating Conditions for Change

Failure in change strategies need not be inevitable. In fact, it is avoidable if change leaders will balance their sense of urgency with a more thoughtful approach to implementing change. If we have learned anything about effective change in schools or any complex organization, it is that neither managerial imperatives nor inspirational speeches will be sufficient to move people and organizations from their entrenched positions. Fortunately, there are practical steps that leaders can take to maximize their probabilities of success.

In Chapter 1, we first suggest that leaders must identify what they can *stop* doing before asking their colleagues to take on a new change initiative. Leaders must also assess with diligence the readiness to change their organizations—and themselves. Change initiatives without such individual and collective assessment are doomed. Chapters 2 and 3 offer Change Readiness Assessments for individuals and organizations, respectively. For an even more extensive analysis of system change readiness, review Appendix A, which contains reproducible forms for analysis of change readiness for every stakeholder.

Chapter 4 presents four imperatives of cultural change, beginning with the counterintuitive suggestion that the first rule of change, particularly when deep cultural change is required, is that leaders must identify and communicate what does *not* change. Although many leaders can eloquently describe their vision of the future and convey genuine optimism and hope, they nevertheless fail to grasp the fear and anxiety that change—even positive and necessary change—creates among their colleagues. Anxiety displaces the advantages of change with overwhelming, if irrational, disadvantages and therefore stops change before it has the opportunity to begin. See if these reactions to change proposals sound familiar:

- "I know that the faculty needs more time for collaboration, but if I give up my role in leading faculty meetings, nobody will know who I am and the faculty won't get the essential information I deliver in these meetings!"

- "I know that our academic expectations of students are inconsistent and ineffective, but if we allow the establishment of standards, then it's the first step toward the federal government taking over the local schools."

- "I know that our present grading system isn't working well, but if we change our grading system, then our children won't have transcripts and they won't get into college!"

- "I know that the way we assign our least experienced and least qualified teachers to our most needy students doesn't make any sense, but if we change our teacher assignment system, then we'll lose everything we have fought for in the union for 30 years!"

- "I know that our board meetings last until 1:00 a.m. and that we have had four superintendents in three years, but if we change the way we run our board meetings, we'll lose the voice of citizen democracy in our schools and the bureaucrats will take over!"

- "I know that vaccinations have saved generations from polio and diphtheria and protect millions of children from communicable diseases, but we can't require vaccinations because there's a chance that my child's illness was caused by vaccinations."

The common theme in each of these reactions is that change leads to loss—not just any loss, but a devastating and personal loss. Opposition to change spreads like a virus, and the irrational fears of a few are quickly transmuted into mob rule. I have witnessed even the most benign reforms, such as the correction of mathematical errors in grading systems, stopped in their tracks because superintendents or boards were unwilling to confront irrational opposition to change. Find a change—any change, no matter how essential—and you'll find opposition to it.

This is hardly unique to education; in fact, opposition to change is embedded deep in the human psyche. Intelligent and rational people are alcoholics and anorexics (and victims of a host of other diseases associated with behavior). They know that their illnesses devastate their lives and the lives of those around them. Nevertheless, they persist in the behaviors associated with their illnesses, often based on the fear that if they stop drinking or starving themselves (or overeating, smoking, snorting cocaine—the list is a long one), then the people who loved them in the past will abandon them. Change means loss; loss means abandonment. Deutschman (2007) notes that while humans rationally associate change as a vital part of life, we nevertheless crave continuity and consistency. We like to think that our conception of our personal identity does not change direction with the wind but rather remains stable over time. The loss of this sense of individuality is threatened by change even, as Deutschman notes, when the change is tremendously positive. Thus change is defeated by anxiety almost every time. In fact, he concludes, the odds against change—even when change is literally a matter of life and death—are a staggering nine to one.

The anxiety that opposes change is not addressed with speeches or memoranda. It is not enough that the leader is a self-proclaimed Change Agent. Rather, psychologists suggest a useful strategy in "reframing" issues that create irrational anxiety (Burns, 1999; Deutschman, 2007). Successful reframing depends on placing the new behaviors into perspective by identifying what does *not* change. Rather than proclaiming that "I'm here to change the entire culture" or "We're about to engage in massive change"—both announcements that are profoundly counterproductive—the effective change leader will look at the qualities, values, and stories that can be reaffirmed. For example, even in schools that are clearly candidates for a turnaround, the wise change leader will begin by asking the faculty, "Who in this room is the first in your family to graduate from college?" In almost every group of educators to whom I have asked the question, more than half of the people respond affirmatively. "What a great story you have to tell! The first in your family to graduate from college! You are models, and I know that I can learn from you and that our students can learn from you." Change leaders will also review specific examples of kindness, caring, and compassion that must be acknowledged and preserved. They will reaffirm the values of respect and fairness. They will, in brief, reframe change from an overwhelming and pervasive threat, to a modification of practice within the broader picture of affirming every colleague as a worthwhile professional and person. This is not a semantic game, but a profound leadership principle. Change leaders know that they do not change organizations without changing individual behavior, and they will not change individual behavior without affirming the people behind the behavior. Here are some examples of how that might sound:

- "Before we talk about changes in our grading system, let's begin with some assurances. We'll still have transcripts, honor rolls, and individualized education plans. We'll still respect your judgment and hard work. We'll still value the thoughtful and constructive feed-back that teachers provide every day. None of that will change."

- "Before we consider changes in course assignment, let's first reaffirm our commitment to our union agreement and the principles of collective bargaining and collaborative decision making. I've been a teacher and a union member, and I know how important these prin-ciples are, and I promise to work with you. That will not change."

- "Before I commit myself to a regimen of diet and exercise, I want to think about my good qualities—the essence of who I am. I was a generous and decent person when I was overweight, and I will continue to be so in the future. That will not change."

When change is reframed from a personal attack to a new, mean-ingful, and exciting opportunity, then the odds in favor of successful change are altered dramatically. Although reframing does not elimi-nate cynicism and doubt by the skeptics, it does provide the leader with space and time to gain trust. Opposition to change remains inevi-table. In fact, if your proposed change does not engender opposition, then you should question whether or not what you are proposing really represents meaningful change. But opposition need not be deadly. When change leaders reframe a change, their essential message is not "You are broken and I am here to fix you." Rather, their message is "You are so valuable and worthy, our mission is so vital, and the future lives of our students are so precious, that we have a joint responsibility to one another to be the best we can be."

Change leaders must examine themselves and their personal examples before they engage in any exhortations for others to change. Howard Gardner (1995) reminds us that leaders influence us most not with their words but with their lives. When a superintendent convenes a mandatory meeting of all school administrators and delivers a well-intended lecture on the evils of mandatory meetings and lectures, then principals can't hear the words through the filter of actions. When a school board claims that their top priority is student achievement and educational equity, but they review the data on these goals only once a year in a deadly dull PowerPoint presentation, with the other 51 meetings devoted to buildings, budgets, and citizen complaints, then the real priorities are evident. When teachers recite the mantra that "all children can learn" but persist in lesson plans, grading policies, and assessments that embody the philosophy that only a few will succeed, then children quickly learn that yet another adult in their lives says one thing and does another. Too many leaders think that their defining moment for effective change will be their speech to employees, their "state of the schools" address to the community, or their remarks to the board of education. But of all the things leaders do in order to create the conditions for change, the most important are their thousands of moments of truth when their actions speak louder than words.

In the final chapter of Part 1, we consider the myths of change leadership. Myths can be convenient and even endearing, as we pass along cherished stories from one generation to the next. I'm quite fond of the Tooth Fairy and Santa Claus, and I have it on good authority that the stork is by far the most convenient method for delivering new babies. Not every myth is so benign, and in Chapter 5, we consider change leadership myths that mislead our stakeholders and undermine our values. Although the evidence challenging these myths is overwhelming, the seductive appeal of leadership change mythology can be staggering. That is the only reason that practices devoid of an evidentiary foundation persist in so many school systems. Only by identifying the myths, confronting the evidence, and presenting clear and compelling alternatives can we ultimately put these tall tales to rest.

1

Pull the Weeds Before You Plant the Flowers

Imagine a gardener who sees row upon row of beautiful flowers in the nursery. He enthusiastically loads a basket to overflowing with annuals and perennials in anticipation of placing each new plant in a special place in the garden. The nursery salesperson is encouraging, explaining that these flowers are special hybrid varieties that research has shown will do well in the local climate. But on arriving home, the gardener faces an unpleasant reality: his garden is full of thistles, crabgrass, dandelions, and other weeds. Here are some choices the gardener might consider:

- Drop the new plants at the threshold of the garden and leave them there, hoping that delivering the plants close to the intended location will be sufficient.
- Plant the new flowers between the weeds, hoping that the nutrients in the soil will support both.
- Give the new plants a stern lecture about "growing smarter" and making wiser use of the available nutrients.
- Pull the weeds. Then, and only then, plant the flowers.

Although the last choice may seem like nothing more than common sense, it is decidedly uncommon in schools. Every education system has weeds. There is not a school district, a school, a department, an office, a job description, or a program that does not have a least a few. If we fail to pull the weeds, we can anticipate conversations like these:

- "We'll have professional learning communities—just as soon as we finish making announcements at the faculty meeting."
- "We'll do common scoring of student work—just as soon as all members of the teaching team finish their parent conferences and discipline reports."
- "We're happy to embrace 'writing across the curriculum'—just as soon as we finish covering a curriculum that has never yet been completed within the school year."

Try this simple experiment. Ask your colleagues to list the initiatives and programs that your school has started within the past five years. Then ask them to list the initiatives and programs that have been discontinued as the result of careful evaluation and weeding. I have never been in a school where the first list is not significantly longer than the second.

Educators are drowning under the weight of initiative fatigue—attempting to use the same amount of time, money, and emotional energy to accomplish more and more objectives. That strategy, fueled by various mixtures of adrenaline, enthusiasm, and intimidation, might work in the short term. But eventually, each initiative added to the pile creates a dramatic decline in organizational effectiveness. As the academic growing season continues, we should not be surprised when some of the new flowers are choked by the omnipresent weeds.

Fortunately, there is an answer to initiative fatigue, and that is the common sense of the gardener. The strategic leader must have a "garden party" to pull the weeds before planting the flowers.

Some school principals have a simple rule—they will introduce no new program until they remove at least one or two existing activities, plans, units, or other time-consumers. These principals have time during faculty meetings for collaborative scoring of student work because they stopped making announcements at such meetings and committed every possible administrative communication to e-mail or written notes instead. Teachers have time for students to do more writing in science and social studies because a team of educators identified the standards that matter the most (Ainsworth, 2003) and made a deliberate decision not to engage in frantic and ineffective coverage of the entire text. Faculty teams make a game of it, finding weeds that seemed small when they started but that collectively were robbing students and teachers of one of their most precious resources—time.

Of course, one person's weed may be another person's flower. Moreover, intense accountability pressures can create a situation in which teachers believe that if a topic might be on the state test, then they must be able to show an accusing administrator that their class covered the topic. Although Marzano, Kendall, and Cicchinelli (1999) demonstrated that adequate coverage of many states' standards would require more than twice the number of classroom hours than are typically available, many schools steadfastly refuse to discard anything—or at least to admit that they do. Thus we are left with curriculum by default; we proceed at a moderate pace through the fall, pick it up to a canter by the winter, gallop through the spring, and still have material left at the end of the year that we did not have time to cover.

Research and common sense make it clear that initiative fatigue is rife in schools. We must identify some things we can stop doing. To begin the weeding process, consider the following three ideas.

1. Use intergrade dialogue to find the essentials. Ask me as a 3rd grade teacher what I am willing to give up, and I may say, "Nothing! Everything I do is important!" But ask the same 3rd grade teacher to tell a colleague in 2nd grade what 2nd grade students should know and be able to do in order to enter the 3rd grade with confidence and success, and the 3rd grade teacher will provide a list that is brief, balanced, and precise. I have asked this question of hundreds of teachers, and not a single time has one said, "For students to enter my 3rd grade classroom confidently next year, the 2nd grade teacher must cover every single state standard." Rather, the teachers giving advice to their colleagues in the next-lower grades provide specific and succinct advice. Entire school districts can conduct this exercise, and they will find high levels of agreement on the essentials, casting doubt on the necessity of some of the more idiosyncratic elements of the curriculum.

2. Sweat the small stuff. We can recover hours of valuable instruction time when teachers share their best time-saving tips. Within the same school, some teachers have transitions among centers that require almost five minutes, while their colleague across the hall accomplishes the same transition in under 20 seconds. Some secondary teachers collect homework as students walk in the door, saving several minutes of classroom time. Some elementary schools have fewer but longer science periods so that teachers lose a smaller percentage of class time setting up and taking down labs. Some technology teachers ensure that every computer is turned on and ready for log-in before students enter the room. These small matters take seconds or minutes during the day, but collectively they amount to exceptionally large time savings.

3. Set the standard for a weed-free garden. Respect the time of teachers: start and end meetings on time, never make routine announcements aloud, and cancel or shorten meetings that are not contributing to student achievement. If leaders will not pull the schoolwide weeds in meetings, conferences, and interruptions, they can hardly ask teachers to weed the classroom gardens.

Leaders at every level might want to try this experiment. At the next gathering of educators, raise your right hand and take the pledge: "I will not ask you to implement one more initiative until we first take some things off the table." Then listen. It might be the first round of applause you've had in a while.

2

The Personal Change
Readiness Assessment

You know more about change leadership than you might think. Although the stories of other people and organizations in later chapters may be useful to you, one of the most important lessons of this book is that *your* stories of successful change are the most compelling. In *Becoming a Resonant Leader*, McKee, Boyatzis, and Johnston (2008) challenge readers to become active participants in learning rather than passive readers of the text. "The act of writing is a very important step in this process," they contend. "Writing causes us to think harder and more deeply, which will provide you with profound insights that will serve you well" (p. 3). Their conclusions build on a wealth of research on adult learning, the consistent conclusion of which is that effective learning requires engagement and personal application. The self-assessment in this chapter opens these essential doors.

Consider three personal changes that you have made in the past five years. These changes could represent a strategic or behavioral change at work, or a change in your personal life, such as an improvement in your diet, exercise routine, or personal relationships. You will be asked to evaluate each change on various criteria, using a scale of 1 to 10, with 1 representing no evidence of the characteristics described, and 10 representing an exceptional reflection of those characteristics. For example, if the personal change you were considering was a program of professional reading, then a score of 10 for "Planning" might be associated with the fact that you created an extensive list of books, articles, Web sites, and other sources and then carefully prioritized and planned your professional reading program. A score of 10 for "Sense of Urgency" might be associated with the fact that, had you failed to complete the professional reading program, you might lose your job, but if you successfully completed it, you would complete an advanced degree, earn greater professional recognition and financial rewards, and satisfy your psychological craving for new knowledge. With regard to "Personal Support," a score of 10 could be related to the fact that your family and friends knew that for 45 minutes every morning and evening, you would be allowed to work without interruption. They knew that this time was important to you and to them, and that once your 90-minute daily discipline of professional learning was completed, you would be able to devote yourself completely to the interests of your family and friends. When you score a 10 on "Personal Focus," you are able to state with complete integrity that almost without fail, you achieved your professional reading objectives and that even other professional and personal priorities did not prevent the accomplishment of this goal. Finally, when you score a 10 in the "Effect on Results" column, you are able to say that you are a more effective professional and that the achievement of this goal had a clear, measurable, and direct effect on your professional and personal goals.

These descriptions could, of course, make a 10 seem out of reach, but that is precisely the point. Honest 10s are rare, and therefore you should be equally fair in awarding low scores. The very fact that you are reading this book suggests a solid commitment to, and interest in, change; that does not mean that every change effort you have engaged in is successful. Chances are that some have been more successful than others, and that is precisely what this opportunity for personal reflection is all about.

Please take a few minutes to complete the following paragraphs. I know how tempting it is to skip over interactive exercises in books; so trust me, this one is important. This is not only important for you but also important for the school or system you wish to lead. Your personal stories of change will give you credibility and will also help you reflect on how to best lead others.

1. Think of several changes you've made—behavioral, personal, relational, physical, or other changes—in the past five years. Please list them briefly here.

Change #1:

_____

Change #2:

_____

Change #3:

_____

Change #4:

_____

Change #5:

_____

2. Think of the change for which you exercised the greatest degree of *planning*. This means that you identified the steps that you would take and you knew clearly how to make the change. Identify just one change and list some of the most important steps in the planning process.

Change:

_____

Step #1:

_____

Step #2:

_____

Step #3:

_____

Step #4:

_____

Step #5:

_____

3. Think of the change for which you had the greatest *sense of urgency*. Describe why the price of failure was high—much higher than the price of change.

If I failed to make this change, then . . .

_____

_____

If I succeeded in making this change, then . . .

_____

_____

4. Think of the change for which you had the greatest *personal support*. Your friends and family knew that you were making a change, and they supported you completely.

How my family supported me:

_____

_____

How my friends supported me:

_____

_____

5. Think of the change for which you had the greatest *personal focus*. Describe how you devoted time to initiating and maintaining the change despite your busy schedule.

_____

_____

6. Think of the change that had the greatest *effect on results* for you or for your organization. Describe these specific and measurable results in as much detail as you can remember.

As a result of the change I successfully completed, I achieved the following results:

_____

_____

Based on these reflections, complete Figure 2.1, listing the three most important changes in the left-hand column and entering a score of 1 to 10 in the remaining columns. If you have time and are willing to engage in deep introspection, consider each change on every dimension. An easy-to-use computerized reflection journal is available as a free download at www.ChangeLeaders.info.

Figure 2.1 | **Personal Change Readiness Assessment**

Directions: For each change, enter a score of 1 to 10 in each column, with 1 representing no evidence of the characteristic described, and 10 representing an exceptional reflection of that characteristic.

Personal Change	Planning I planned in advance the steps I would take and knew clearly how to make the change.	Sense of Urgency I knew that the price of failing to change was much greater than the price of changing.	Personal Support My family and friends knew I was making a change and supported me.	Personal Focus I devoted time to initiating and maintaining the change despite my busy schedule.	Effect on Results I can measure the results of the change, and they are clear and significant.
1.					
2.					
3.					

Finally, complete your Personal Change Score:

Total for Change #1 _____

Total for Change #2 _____

Total for Change #3 _____

Total for the *two highest changes* _____

In the next chapter, we will explore your organizational change experience and then integrate the two experiences to determine how your personal change and organizational change experiences combine to create a change readiness profile.

3

The Organizational Change Readiness Assessment

In Chapter 2 we considered your personal change experiences. In this chapter we review your experiences with organizational change and then integrate these two sets of experiences to complete your personal Change Readiness Assessment.

Remember, the physical act of writing is important, so please complete all of the work in this chapter, including the written responses and the scoring of your change experiences. If you prefer to enter your responses on a computer, you can complete the Change Readiness Assessment for free by using the online service at www. ChangeLeaders.info.

Consider three organizational changes that you have experienced in the past five years. These changes could represent change in a single team or for the entire organization. Perhaps it involved a strategic plan, a quality improvement, a technology implementation, or other systemic changes. You will be asked to evaluate each change on various criteria, using a scale of 1 to 10, with 1 representing no evidence of the characteristics described and 10 representing an exceptional reflection of those characteristics. For example, if the organizational change you were considering was a technology initiative for improved computer security, then a score of 10 for "Planning" might be associated with the fact that your organization created an extensive list of planning steps, including training, technology support, hardware changes, and personal follow-up for every person who was affected by the change. A score of 10 for "Sense of Urgency" might be associated with the fact that, had you failed to complete the computer security initiative, your organization might lose a great deal of time and money, but if you successfully completed it, you would be able to not only safeguard your computerized information but also accomplish more for a mission you believe to be very important. With regard to "Personal Support," a score of 10 could be related to the fact that your family and friends knew that sometimes this important organizational initiative would require extra time at work and limit your flexibility to spend time with them. They knew that this time was important to you and that once the computer security initiative was completed, you would be able to spend more time with them. When you score a 10 on "Stakeholder Support," you observed comprehensive stakeholder engagement at every level, including elected officials, community members, students, parents, teachers, administrators, and a broad cross section of interest groups that would be affected by the proposed change. Finally, when you score a 10 on "Effect on Results," you are able to say that you and your team were more effective because you are not diverted by the risks, costs, and time required by lapses in computer security.

These descriptions could, of course, make a score of 10 seem out of reach, but that is precisely the point. Honest 10s are rare, and therefore you should be equally fair in awarding low scores. The very fact that you are reading this book suggests a solid commitment to, and interest in, change. That does not mean that every change effort you have engaged in has been successful. Chances are that some have been more successful than others, and that is precisely what this opportunity for personal reflection is all about.

Please take a few minutes to complete the following paragraphs. Again, I ask that you resist the temptation to skip over this interactive exercise and instead recognize its importance—not only for you, but for the school or system you wish to lead. Like the stories of personal change you recorded in Chapter 2, your stories of organizational change will give you credibility and will also help you reflect on how to best lead others.

1. Think of several organizational changes in the past five years that have particular relevance for you. Please list them briefly here.

Change #1:

_____

Change #2:

_____

Change #3:

_____

Change #4:

_____

Change #5:

_____

2. Think of the organizational change for which you exercised the greatest degree of *planning*. This means that you identified the steps

that you would take and you knew clearly how to make the change. Identify just one change and list some of the most important steps in the planning process:

Change:

_____

Step #1:

_____

Step #2:

_____

Step #3:

_____

Step #4:

_____

Step #5:

_____

3. Think of the organizational change for which you had the greatest *sense of urgency*. Describe why the price of failure was high—much higher than the price of change.

If I failed to make this change, then . . .

_____

_____

If I succeeded in making this change, then . . .

_____

_____

4. Think of the organizational change for which you had the greatest *stakeholder support*. Your friends and family knew that your organization was making a change, and they supported you completely.

How organizational stakeholders (employees, leaders, policymakers) supported the proposed organizational change:

_____

_____

How community stakeholders (businesses, senior citizens, parents, and other groups) supported the proposed organizational change:

_____

_____

5. Think of the organizational change for which you had the greatest *leadership focus*. Describe how you devoted time to initiating and maintaining the change despite your busy schedule.

_____

_____

6. Think of the organizational change that had the greatest *effect on results* for you or for your organization. Describe these specific and measureable results in as much detail as you can remember.

As a result of the change I successfully completed, I achieved the following results:

_____

_____

Based on these reflections, complete the Organizational Change Readiness Assessment in Figure 3.1, listing the three most important changes in the left-hand column and entering a score from 1 to 10 for each column, with 10 representing the highest level of change effectiveness. The Organizational Change Readiness Assessment considers the capacity of the organization and the leader to engage in significant change.

Figure 3.1 | **Organizational Change Readiness Assessment**

Directions: For each change, enter a score of 1 to 10 in each column, with 1 representing no evidence of the characteristic described, and 10 representing an exceptional reflection of that characteristic.

Organizational Change	Planning	Sense of Urgency	Stakeholder Support	Leadership Focus	Effect on Results
	Plans were clear, detailed, and effectively communicated.	Widespread sense of the immediate need for change was apparent.	Employees, clients, and the community understood and supported the change.	Senior leadership made the change their clear and consistent focus long after initiation.	The change had a measurable and significant effect on results.
1.					
2.					
3.					

Finally, complete your Organizational Change Score:

Total for Change #1 _____

Total for Change #2 _____

Total for Change #3 _____

Total for the *two highest changes* _____

The total for the two highest changes in your Organizational Change Score represents the *horizontal* score.

Going back to Chapter 2, enter the total for the two highest changes in your Personal Change Score: _____. This total represents the *vertical* score.

Use these two scores to enter an X in the appropriate box of the Change Readiness Matrix (Figure 3.2). For example, if you have a horizontal score of 80 and a vertical score of 70, then you will place an X in the upper right-hand quadrant. If you have a horizontal score of 20 and a vertical score of 60, then you will place an X in the upper left-hand quadrant. (If you prefer to let the computer do this for you, go to www.ChangeLeaders.info and take the Change Readiness Assessment online.)

Figure 3.2 | **Change Readiness Matrix**

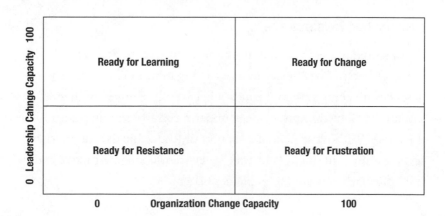

Now that you know the quadrant that best represents your change readiness, let us consider in greater detail the implications of your Change Readiness scores.

Ready for Learning

If you scored in the upper-left quadrant, you are Ready for Learning. Here the leader demonstrates a history of successful change, with a strong capacity for planning and executing change. The organization can learn from the leader's personal and professional example. Before undertaking a new change initiative, however, the leader must attend to the learning needs of the organization. Specifically, the organization may need work on planning, communicating, and executing change. Moreover, the organization must create an evidence-based culture in which a clear and compelling case for change leads to a sense of urgency by every stakeholder. Finally, a commitment to clear and public displays of data must be in place so that the results of the change can be widely shared, reinforcing the commitment and hard work of every person contributing to the change effort.

Ready for Resistance

If you scored in the lower-left quadrant, then you are Ready for Resistance. When neither the leader nor the organization has a history of successful change, then the most likely result of any new change initiative will be resistance, anger, undermining, or simply ignoring the effort. Without stakeholder support or leadership execution, these organizations will simply "out-wait" every new change initiative and the leaders who attempt to implement them.

Ready for Frustration

If you scored in the lower-right corner, then you are Ready for Frustration. When an organization with a strong history of change is led by someone who either is reluctant to engage in systemic change or lacks the personal capacity to do so, then the potential for frustration is strong. Each time the organization gets ahead of the leader and the ensuing change fails to be supported by senior leadership, change becomes less safe. Eventually, the organization will stop taking the risks and migrate to the left-hand side of the matrix. The next leader will inherit an organization with severely compromised change readiness, and it will take time to rebuild trust and regain change capacity.

Ready for Change

If you scored in the upper-right quadrant, then both the leader and the organization have exceptional change capacity, and the organization is a model of resilience. This organization can adapt to environmental and cultural shifts, change strategies and form, innovate services and resources, and create an atmosphere of excitement and engagement.

❋ ❀ ❋ ❀ ❋ ❀

Now that you know your readiness for change, we turn our attention to the factors affecting school culture. Although it is tempting to address such a challenge with the imperatives of what must change, we will consider the counterintuitive principle that the first duty of leadership is defining what does *not* change. Only when you meet your colleagues' needs for stability will you be able to challenge them for successful change.

4

Cultural Change

How do you change the culture of schools? Consider the following recent laments I have heard from school leaders:

- "We can't change the grading policy—it's part of our culture."
- "Public displays of data won't work here—the culture won't allow it."
- "The parents just don't understand—you can't change a hundred years of culture by passing a law."

Although each of these statements includes the word *culture*, the meaning of the term ranges from policies and procedures to personal preferences to deeply embedded belief systems. Although cultural change is challenging and time-consuming, it is not only possible but necessary. This is particularly true in schools and other organizations where the word *culture* is used as a rhetorical talisman to block leadership initiative, to stifle innovation, and to maintain the status quo.

Evidence from schools and other organizations that have experienced successful change provides encouragement for leaders who know that meaningful change begins with cultural change. Two of the foremost change researchers, John Kotter and Holger Rathgeber (1995), suggest that "90 percent of organizations were either ignoring relevant changes or were trying to adjust in ways that were not meeting their aspirations. Too much time and money was being spent to achieve too little, with too much pain and frustration all around" (p. 140). If we have learned anything in the educational standards movement in the last decade, it is that policy change without cultural change is an exercise in futility and frustration.

Culture Defined

Because the very term *culture* has so many different meanings, let us begin with a definition of terms. In the context of school change, we might define *culture* as simply "the way we do things around here." *Merriam-Webster's Collegiate Dictionary* (1998) hardly leaps to the same conclusion, relegating to the fifth definition of *culture* the phrase "behavior typical of a group or class."

What is the culture of your school or district? It is not likely to be found in lofty vision statements, missions, or strategic planning documents. Culture is reflected in the behavior, attitudes, and beliefs of individuals and groups. The single greatest impediment to meaningful cultural change is the gap between what leaders say that they value and what leaders actually value. Staff members are not seduced by a leader's claim of "collaborative culture" when every meeting is a series of lectures, announcements, and warnings. The assertion of a "creative culture" is contradicted by a practice of unbending uniformity. Claims about a "culture of high expectations" are undermined by the encouragement of good grades for poor student work. A "culture of respect" is undermined by every imperious, demanding, and angry e-mail and voice mail. Mottoes proclaiming a "culture of equity" are fraudulent when essential interventions to improve student performance are sacrificed on the altar of traditional schedules and the convenience of adults.

Four Imperatives of Cultural Change

Leaders have a broad range of advice for implementing change strategies, much of it unburdened by evidence to support the platitudes. When it comes to profound and lasting cultural change, however, there are four essentials that are consistent across many leadership contexts, including education, business, government, and nonprofit organizations.

First, leaders must *define what will not change.* They must articulate the values, practices, traditions, and relationships that will *not* be lost. Rather than make every change a bruising personal battle that exhausts political capital, diminishes trust, and creates the toxic atmosphere of "either you're with us or against us," effective change leaders must place change in the context of stability. Although "the only constant is change" might make a good sound bite, the connotation of such a statement is "whatever you have been doing in the past I have adjudged to be ineffective, and your experience and professional judgment are irrelevant." For leaders who wish to overcome the cultural impediments to change, a more thoughtful statement might be this: "I know that change is exceptionally difficult, and therefore I am only going to ask you to engage in changes that I know will have meaning and value for you and every stakeholder we serve." Be specific—identify those values, traditions, and practices that you will preserve, not just those that you will change.

Second, *organizational culture will change with leadership actions*; speeches and announcements are not enough. Heifetz and Linsky (2002) refer to the most challenging changes as "adaptive" and note that these challenges "cannot be solved by someone who provides answers from on high. Without learning new ways—changing attitudes, values, and behaviors—people cannot make the adaptive leap necessary to thrive in the new environment" (p. 13). Leaders speak most clearly with their actions—changes they make in decision rules (who has the authority to make what decisions), allocation of personal time (meetings accepted and canceled), and relationships (taking the time to understand the personal stories of colleagues). When staff members hear the clarion call for transformation from a leader whose personal actions have remained unchanged, their hope turns to cynicism in an instant.

Third, *use the right change tools for your system*. Christensen, Marx, and Stevenson (2006) differentiate "culture tools," such as rituals and traditions; "power tools," such as threats and coercion; "management tools," such as training, procedures, and measurement systems; and "leadership tools," including role modeling and vision. Leaders must choose the appropriate change tools based on a combination of factors, including the extent to which staff members agree on what they want and their consensus on cause and effect. "The same actions viewed as inspiring and visionary" by some employees "can be regarded with indifference or disdain" by others (Christensen et al., 2006, p. 77). Leaders who come to their position with a particular method of creating change make the mistake of the person who holds a hammer and who thus sees only nails. To change the collective behaviors and beliefs of the complex organizations we call schools, leaders must apply the right combination of change tools, varying their strategies to meet the changing needs of the system.

Fourth, *change in culture requires relentless personal attention and "scut work" by the leader*. In one of the most compelling examples of cultural change in modern times, Dr. Paul Farmer revolutionized the beliefs and practices of stakeholders ranging from the poorest rural villagers in Haiti to the faculty of the Harvard Medical School to policymakers at the United Nations (Kidder, 2004). Combining his extensive field experience with sophisticated research and medical analyses, Farmer upended traditional notions of health care initially in Haiti and ultimately in the entire world. He reveals that one of his secrets to profound change is the willingness of leaders to do "unglam-orous scut work." Adds Farmer, "[The] reluctance to do scut work is why a lot of my peers don't stick with this kind of work." Although educational leaders must spend time making speeches and attending board meetings, the leaders aspiring to cultural change will take the risk, as Superintendent Stan Scheer of the Murrieta Valley Unified School District in California has done, of taking a turn as a substitute teacher and spending time with bus drivers at five o'clock on a frosty morning. No doubt some leaders will insist that every job has value and there is no such thing as "scut work" in schools. If so, then back up those words with personal example and public actions.

5

Confronting the Myths
of Change Leadership

Wander into any bookstore and find the section labeled "Leadership,"
and you'll see a host of historical figures whom you are directed to
emulate: Elizabeth I, Moses, Catherine the Great, Henry Ford, Attila
the Hun—the list is endless. Never mind that the list includes one of
the foremost figures of Judaism and a notorious anti-Semite, along with
monarchs and barbarians who engaged in bloodlust, torture, and con-
quest. They were leaders who certainly created change, and, because
they are conveniently absent from the scene, they can be used as props
in the latest psychobabble about change leadership. It is less popular
but more constructive for our purposes to deconstruct some of the
popular myths of change leadership, and that is the task of this chapter.

Calling something a "myth" is not necessarily pejorative. Many
belief systems, for example, share similar myths for creation, the
seasons, the weather, and the development of the human species.
Although myths may be manufactured for convenience (I can't think
of another reason for the bilious suggestion that Attila was a leader to
be emulated), other myths endure because they provide explanations
for a phenomenon that can be challenging and confusing. Moreover,

myths that are widely accepted take on a life of their own through repetition, if not through rigorous inquiry.

If the Leadership section of the bookstore were really to have a book that synthesized the modern mythology of leadership, the title would be *Leadership by Narcissus: How to Achieve Greatness by Being Obsessed with Yourself*. Truth in labeling, of course, is not the hallmark of retail sales, so you are unlikely to see such a title in a bookstore anytime soon. However, if the substance of a book, particularly its pretensions of historical scholarship, leads the reader to narcissism rather than teamwork, then *caveat emptor*—let the buyer beware.

In this chapter, we consider seven popular myths of leadership:

- Myth #1: Plan your way to greatness.
- Myth #2: Just a little bit better is good enough.
- Myth #3: We want you to change us . . . *really*.
- Myth #4: People love to collaborate.
- Myth #5: Hierarchy changes systems.
- Myth #6: Volume equals VOLUME.
- Myth #7: The leader is the perfect composite of every trait.

Myth #1: Plan Your Way to Greatness

Perhaps the most pervasive myth in change leadership is that planning —particularly complex, large-scale, and supposedly "strategic" planning —leads to effective change. As Chapter 9 suggests, the evidence for that proposition is absent not only in education but in the business world as well. In an evaluation of school plans, for example, my colleagues at the Leadership and Learning Center learned that student proficiency was dramatically higher (46.3 percent compared with 25.6 percent, as expressed by the average percent proficient on tests from elementary through high school) when comparing schools with the lowest scores on plan format to schools with the highest scores on plan format. That is not a misprint; schools that excelled in format had lower achievement. Thus, the emphasis that schools placed on excellent formatting was worse than a waste of time; it was *inversely* related to student achievement.

If you must have a plan, then learn from the schools that have done it well. Establish clear vision and values, expressing who you are and who you are not. If you can't write your mission and values on the back of your business card and you can't say them without reference to notes, then they are not influencing your daily reality. Appendix B provides an example of a "Plan on a Page," in which a school system with a long track record of improved achievement and equity expressed its commitment to a clear mission, vision, and goals on a single page.

Myth #2: Just a Little Bit Better Is Good Enough

Perhaps a few readers will remember Andy Taylor, the amiable sheriff of Mayberry, played by Andy Griffith, star of the eponymous television show. When he was not dealing with Barney, Opie, Aunt Bee, and Otis in his comedic role, Griffith made his living as a pitchman for a cereal company, assuring us that his product was "just a little bit better." His model has a distinguished line of descendents in leadership consultants who suggest that successful firms do not do one thing much better but do many things just a little bit better (Peters & Waterman, 1982). This incremental approach has been endorsed more recently by legions of people who believe, with abundant sincerity but a paucity of evidence, that small changes by the enthusiastic few will change the system. They earnestly quote Margaret Mead: "Never doubt that a small group of committed individuals can change the world; indeed, it is the only thing that ever has."

In fact, small groups do not change schools. The salient variable for multiple programs is not their brand name or content, but the degree to which they are implemented in schools (Reeves, 2008, 2009). Rather than acknowledge that the incremental approach itself is deeply flawed, the most common response of senior leadership is to abandon the first ineffective incremental change and replace it with yet another incremental change effort, followed by the same incomplete and ineffective implementation. Although the hope is that achievement will improve incrementally as implementation improves, the evidence does not sustain this hope. In fact, in surprising research, we found that for many change initiatives, implementation that was moderate or occasional was no better than implementation that was completely absent. Only deep implementation had the desired effect on student achievement.

"Just a little bit better" is appealing because it suggests that the change initiative need only appeal to those who embraced it—those who attended the conference, read the book, heard the speaker, or were already engaged in the change before the leader requested it. Deep and sustainable change, by contrast, requires changes in behavior among those who do not welcome the change. In ancient and contemporary societies, myths persist because they transfer responsibility from ourselves to external forces beyond our control. As long as we believe the myth that incremental change will work, we do not have to engage in the unpleasant task of implementing change, and we avoid the difficult truth that behavior precedes belief—that is, most people must engage in a behavior before they accept that it is beneficial; then they see the results, and then they believe that it is the right thing to do. Certainly the payoffs are there when leaders take the initiative and achieve high levels of implementation, but as this book demonstrates in case after case, the implementation precedes buy-in; it does not follow it.

Myth #3: We Want You to Change Us . . . *Really*

Educational leaders, particularly those at senior levels, are often implored to become change leaders. The board members who hire them stress the need for a new direction, and their subordinates willingly talk about the flaws of the previous leader. Change in the superintendent, chief academic officer, or other senior position, they reason, is at last an opportunity to create meaningful change. In truth, what they mean is that this is an opportunity for *other people* to change. The same board members who demanded that the new superintendent create change are shocked when they discover that part of the change the new superintendent has in mind will include adjustments in the same board members' pet programs. The same cabinet members who expected that, at a minimum, change would bring the opportunity to put their competitors in the endless game of organizational politics in their place are dismayed to find that part of the change the new leader has in mind is not a different set of winners and losers, but a change in the game itself.

In truth, any change will meet resistance, because change is loss. In fact, meaningful change is a particular kind of loss. Are the following stages familiar to you?

- Denial
- Anger
- Bargaining
- Depression
- Acceptance

These are, of course, the stages of grief described by Dr. Elisabeth Kübler-Ross (1969). Even the most productive and essential changes represent the death of past practice; therefore, for people to have genuine enthusiasm for change, we must believe that they have an enthusiasm for death and loss—a premise that demands challenge. In almost every case I have observed in thousands of schools on five continents, the kind of change for which people have the greatest enthusiasm is change directed at other people, other practices, and other institutions. I cannot say that I recall a single example of genuine and sustained enthusiasm for change when the one claiming enthusiasm is the one who is also grieving the loss of past practices and all of the emotional and psychological gains that those past practices brought. These losses are the same whether we are giving up the taste of the extra helping of bacon, the third martini, or the flexing of academic power that comes with long-practiced grading, teaching, and leadership practices. Change is loss, and leaders who do believe in the myth of the popularity of change had better start searching for the Change Fairy.

Myth #4: People Love to Collaborate

What could be better than collaboration? We are social animals, after all, and anyone who has observed teachers as they assemble each fall can testify to the genuine enthusiasm with which they greet one another, share stories, and re-form their personal relationships. However, there is, as Roland Barth (1990) reminds us, a difference between congeniality and collegiality. The former is important and can provide the social lubricant that allows people to work together under stressful circumstances. But it is not the same as the difficult and challenging work of collaboration. To be effective, professional collaboration requires time, practice, and accountability. Schools that claim, for example, to be professional learning communities but fail to provide time for collaboration are engaging in self-delusion. But those schools that provide generous amounts of time—in some cases 45 to

60 minutes three to five times each week—but fail to provide practice and accountability for effective collaboration are equally delusionary, though they can engage in the fantasy of collaboration at a more leisurely pace.

Collaboration can take many forms, from the focus on an individual student to the development of multidisciplinary lessons to the analysis of recent achievement data. Every collaboration meeting, however, must have defined results with specific and measureable adult actions. Just as students should be able to articulate, "If I learn this lesson well, I should be able to . . . ," so, too, educators and administrators should be able to say, "If this meeting is successful, then we should be able to . . . ."

Consider the example of collaborative scoring of student work. This topic is a good place to begin collaborative efforts because it gets at the very heart of the transformation of academic expectations into the daily reality of student work. In one case, I asked 50 teachers to evaluate several samples of student work, a process that allowed me to calculate the degree of agreement or disagreement after my professional development efforts. A high degree of agreement would reflect the effectiveness of my instruction in standards and assessment. In addition to considering the level of agreement among the teachers, I could also evaluate the speed with which they came to agreement on each piece of work.

The results were illuminating, particularly for a professional developer operating under the influence of the myth that if I delivered a seminar with sufficient enthusiasm and wit, then the teachers in the audience were better served by listening to my wisdom than by engaging in the hard work of practicing what they learned. Authors, too, must sacrifice their myths. This quickly became evident when, after six hours of a terrifically inspiring lecture on the value of standards, assessment, and collaboration, I gave samples of student work to the 50 teachers and calculated the results. With a four-point scale, one might think that the lowest score possible for collaboration on an assignment would be 25 percent, with a quarter of participating teachers selecting each of the four possible student marks. Thus it took math-defying incompetence for me to conclude that the mean level of agreement was only 19 percent, a score that was possible only because some participants, given splendid instruction, crystal clear rubrics, and abundant time, could not come to any conclusion about the work.

It gets worse. I calculated the time it took each group to finish each collaborative scoring assignment, and the average time was a bit less than 45 minutes. I not only did a terrible job; I took a long time to do a terrible job. The disagreements among the participants became, at times, angry and emotional. Their supposed enthusiasm for a day of professional collaboration disintegrated into a sullen wait for the day's seminar to end.

This is the critical juncture in any collaborative effort. If your goal is popularity, then you are finished, and professional collaboration will meet the same fate as every other change that failed because the true standard was popularity, rather than effectiveness. If, however, you are committed to effective change, then persistence through the initial challenges to achieve the essential short-term wins will be necessary, even when that persistence is unpopular.

Collaboration requires practice, not merely instruction. Effective change does not happen with seminars and speeches, but with effective and repeated practice of the professional behaviors that you expect to change. In the case of this seminar in effective assessment, the same 50 educators with the same students and the same staff developer continued to hone their collaboration skills. It was not my instruction but their willingness to engage in focused practice that improved their level of agreement—after approximately 18 additional hours of work (24 professional development hours in total)—from 19 percent to 92 percent. The same group improved not only the accuracy and consistency of their assessment of student work but also their speed, reducing the time required to evaluate the work from 45 minutes to 9 minutes.

Consider offering the following challenge to your colleagues: "This will be difficult and challenging work. It's going to take time and practice. But if you hang in there with me, we will not only improve the quality and consistency of our feedback to students, but we will also save time by dramatically accelerating the speed with which we can collaboratively score student work."

Effective collaboration is not something that people seek or particularly enjoy—at least not in the early stages. Rather, the practices are sustained because the leader develops evidence of effectiveness. Although I cannot say that collaborative scoring is a universally popular practice, it is undeniably true that every faculty in the world appreciates the opportunity to save time. Moreover, even the most cynical observer would acknowledge that a faculty that provides feedback with a consistency level of 92 percent will be perceived by students, parents, and colleagues as more fair and effective than a faculty whose level of consistency is less than 20 percent.

Myth #5: Hierarchy Changes Systems

Governments, educational organizations, and schools themselves are hierarchical organizations. Although the original "principal" was, in fact, the "principal teacher" who led by example and was, first and foremost, a teacher, today's principal is widely expected to be both the instructional leader of the school and the administrative manager. For readers who reject the "manager" title, I gently, respectfully, and firmly suggest that you examine today's task list along with the contents of your inbox and desktop. Count the number of tasks, pieces of paper, and priorities screaming for your attention that are best categorized as management of people, projects, and paper and those that are better categorized as instructional leadership. If the former outnumber the latter, it does not mean that you are unable or unwilling to be an instructional leader, but it suggests that it is unwise to abjure the responsibilities of management.

The role of the hierarchy in organizational change is typically to communicate the essential message of change. This appealing theory, when applied to school change, embraces the "telephone" effect, named after the children's game in which a story is whispered around the room from one child to the next, with diminishing degrees of accuracy. In the adult version of the game, the superintendent whispers to the deputy, who then whispers the same—or almost the same—story to the assistant superintendent. The story—or a pretty close variation of it—is repeated to principals who pass it along—or something fairly close—to the assistant principals, who, if they have time, will attempt to recall what they heard to department heads and grade-level leaders, who may share it with faculty members. Months later, the superintendent is shocked to learn that the change initiative that was crystal clear when she first announced it is, at the classroom level, shrouded in mystery or wildly distorted.

Am I exaggerating? Here are examples I have observed personally in my work in schools. What began as a superintendent's effort to improve the relevance of homework and associate it with more direct feedback from the teacher was transmuted, within days, into the claim by more than one employee that "we aren't allowed to give homework anymore." An attempt to suggest that grades should be linked to student academic proficiency became "we won't have transcripts and letter grades anymore." The suggestion that a school should evaluate student achievement against academic content standards became "we're going back to psychological tests and value judgments of outcomes-based education." In other cases, what district leaders regarded as consistent and nonnegotiable literacy programs varied wildly from one school to another. Assessment practices that were consistent and uniform one year became fragmented and ineffective after only a few changes in key administrative assignments at the building and district levels.

The alternative to hierarchy is not the absence of administrative leadership. Superintendents, principals, and other administrative leaders are necessary but insufficient elements of change leadership. Networks of teachers and administrators offer a powerful and fast method of communication, sharing effective practice, responding to change-lings, and providing practical insights in a way that administrative hierarchies cannot do. In the recent book *Change Wars*, Hargreaves and Fullan (2009) and I (Reeves, 2009) provide examples of how networks can influence the direction, scope, and complexity of change that vastly exceeds that of traditional hierarchy. Their examples come from diverse settings, including education, the military, international finance, and medicine. Three contemporary examples further illuminate the power of networks.

First, the Connecticut Department of Education has conducted an annual "science fair" for the past three years. It is a remarkable event at which the state superintendent, state school board president, and state teacher's union president unanimously endorse the idea of teachers networking with teachers. The remarkably varied examples of effective practice provide a direct link, teacher to teacher, that would otherwise have been dozens of "degrees of separation" from the original idea in Bristol to the teacher who could apply the same idea in Hartford. Similar networks have been established in Virginia, Nevada, Texas, and California.

Second, the Wallace Foundation has supported networks of superintendents in intensive long-term reflection (www.wallacefoundation.

org/elan). Elmore (2009) reports the remarkable impact of consistent and sustained communication among superintendents who are otherwise disconnected from opportunities for improved practice.

Third, there are a growing number of noncommercial Web-based networks designed to allow educational leaders to exchange ideas, debate concepts, and engage in direct contact without hierarchy boundaries. Examples include www.EdTrust.org, where a search engine provides direct access to the details on student achievement in schools that are demographically similar to the school of the person making the inquiry, and www.AllThingsPLC.info, where participants can share ideas, download useful tools, and get personal feedback from researchers and authors, all without a single pop-up advertisement or sales solicitation. With the publication of this book, the commerce-free www.ChangeLeaders.info will join those ranks, providing educators around the world with the opportunity to share ideas and communicate directly. I have described "Level 5 Networks" as those that are sustained not by hierarchical imperative but by shared values. When resources are tight and anxiety levels are high, the essential question is this: Will this network be sustained without budgetary support or administrative mandates? My conclusion is not that hierarchy is irrelevant but that it is inherently limited by time and resources. Even the most benevolent monarch will perish, and the most generous budget will encounter a downturn in the economic cycle. Sustainable change, therefore, is a function not of a willful authority figure but of a shared value system.

Myth #6: Volume Equals VOLUME

If there is a consistent theme in the research on organizational change, it is that opposition is inevitable and the search for universal buy-in is a chimera. This does not validate the leader who runs roughshod over opposition, but it does require that opposition be placed into perspective. Leaders will never, for example, get 100 percent of the faculty to enjoy professional collaboration, particularly when some faculty members define their professional independence, self-respect, and personal identity precisely in terms of not having to collaborate. In fact, they take a good deal of pride in being the only teacher to require this or the most demanding faculty member when it comes to that. Consistency to them is not a sign of fairness but of mediocrity. In these cases, the goal of the leader is not to ask the faculty member to enjoy collaboration, but rather to cooperate in collaborative efforts.

Before spending too much time on the opposition, it is useful to quantify it. In *The Learning Leader* (Reeves, 2006b), I published the results of surveys of 2,000 teachers and administrators. Since that time, we have added an additional 4,000 respondents to the database, but the results have not changed. On more than a dozen different change initiatives, we find that 17 percent of teachers were willing to lead the effort, assisting their colleagues, sharing their knowledge, and facilitating professional learning. An additional 53 percent were willing to model the change efforts in their classrooms, allowing others to observe their efforts. The third category, "fence-sitters," were aware of the change initiative but had not yet implemented it, and they made up 28 percent of the sample. That leaves 2 percent—the Toxic 2 percent— who were either defiantly unaware of leadership expectations or, more likely, actively opposed them. The Toxic 2 can make quite a bit of noise, thus perpetuating the myth that their "VOLUME," as a measure of the organizational decibels that they generate, is the same as their "volume," a rational quantification of their relative numbers among the faculty. The challenge for every time-starved leader is how to spend time and which faculty members to engage. The evidence suggests that leaders are better advised to lavish their time, appreciation, and support on 70 percent of faculty—the 17 percent who are leaders and the 53 percent who are models—rather than continue to engage in ineffective and emotionally draining combat with the Toxic 2.

Myth #7: The Leader Is the Perfect Composite of Every Trait

We return to the bookstore section on Leadership, populated not only by volumes about barbarians and faux histories of monarchs, but also by thoughtful reviews of exceptional women and men who were extraordinary leaders. Although we can certainly learn from the lives of Harriet Tubman and George Washington, Martin Luther King Jr. and Simón Bolívar, Abraham Lincoln and Susan B. Anthony, we are poorly advised to compare our leadership efforts to these historical ideals. In fact, for every historical biography of a great leader, there are thousands of untold stories of unnamed team members, colleagues, friends, and family who contributed to the successes of those whose pictures adorn the covers of even the best leadership studies. The myth is not that these people led lives worthy of study, but rather that our greatest lesson should be the formation of a singular leadership composite. The complexities of change leadership require not the perfect composite of every trait, but rather a team that exhibits leadership traits and exercises leadership responsibilities in a way that no individual leader, past or present, possibly could.

※ ◉ ※ ◉ ※ ◉ ※ ◉

By considering leadership myths, our purpose is not to criticize and destroy, but to create constructive alternatives. We can develop leaders whose focus and vision prevent them from believing that plans are a substitute for action. We can nurture leaders who understand that deep implementation, not a timid incremental approach, is essential for systemic change. We can protect leaders from the seductive allure of those whose enthusiasm for change extends only to others but never to themselves. We can provide time, patience, and support for leaders to create opportunities for collaboration that is meaningful and effective. We can participate in networks and thereby create change in a manner that is faster and more effective than change filtered through hierarchy alone. We can label the Toxic 2 for what it is, a tiny minority that creates noise far out of proportion to the number of stakeholders it represents. And most of all, we can participate in a leadership team, relieving both the senior leader and the organization of the myth that perfection in leadership exists or should be sought.

The rest of this book is about the imperfect work of groups of imperfect people who nevertheless seek to implement and sustain change that will bring their organizations closer to their ideals and values.

PART 2

Planning Change

If ever an oxymoron were worthy of the name, it is a phrase with almost any combination of the words *planning* and *change*. For anyone who has endured mind-numbing worship ceremonies before an altar of three-ring binders under the guise of strategic planning, the great temptation will be to skip this section altogether. Let me make a brief case for why the following chapters are worth your time.

First, we begin in Chapter 6 with a consideration of the few leverage points that have the greatest influence on student achievement: teaching, professional learning, collaboration, and time (including meetings). Whenever a leader says, "We believe in your research and we'll do whatever you ask—as long as we don't have to change the schedule, course assignments, or professional practices of the faculty," then I know that the commitment to research is rhetorical rather than real. These are the leaders who claim to engage in professional learning communities but, in fact, have only changed the name of their faculty meetings.

Next, we consider the truth that leaders seeking to change organizations must also change people. This task is much easier when the right people are selected in the first place. In Chapter 7 we look at some unusual but highly effective ways of interviewing and selecting teachers and administrators. However effective new employees may be, they need nurturing and support. One common method of supporting professionals is coaching, and in Chapter 8 we consider the right way and the wrong way to coach for improved performance.

Finally, in Chapter 9 we consider the sensitive subject of strategic planning. You already know that you can't do it all, and you are rightfully suspicious of planning processes that proceed from vision to mission to endless strategies accompanied by action plans that are, in fact, strategies to avoid action. You already know that effective planning for change requires choices and frequent use of the word *no*—alien concepts in processes that are dominated by the pooling of opinions, earnest listening, and frenzied writing on poster-size paper.

Although leaders must, in fact, listen to a variety of constituencies and should listen courteously to a variety of opinions—however unencumbered by data those opinions may be—leaders must also be relentlessly focused. The research in this section suggests that to have the maximum effect on student achievement, educational leaders must monitor just a few areas. The proliferation of goals and strategies is inversely related to the ability of leaders to monitor them. Therefore, as White (2009) has suggested, when school leaders have more than half a dozen goals, they tend to lose focus and ultimately abandon their ability to monitor the performance of their organization.

Of course, everyone already knows that we need to focus. But what we know and what we do diverge wildly in schools and many other organizations. My observations in thousands of schools suggest that focus is rare and, in some cases, contrary to mandates from external authorities. I have personally read three different school district plans with more than 200 discrete goals, each of which were to be monitored and measured—at least in the fantasies of the people designing the plans. My colleagues at the Leadership and Learning Center have reviewed more than 2,000 school plans, with many of them sporting more than 50 separate goals—again with the hope that each will be monitored and measured. That's 50 goals (and in some cases more than 70) for an individual school. Worse yet, many states *require* the proliferation of goals in the hope that mandatory goals for a variety of different worthy initiatives will lead to the accomplishment of those initiatives. The problem is that there is no evidentiary foundation for goal proliferation; in fact, the evidence points in the opposite direction.

If you are a state, provincial, or national policymaker, how would you like to be the leader who becomes a hero by reducing planning requirements? How would you like to say to your stakeholders, "I'm here today not to announce a new initiative or mandate, but to announce the following list of requirements that you do *not* need to follow. We've conducted some research and found that a few of the things we have asked you to do actually lead to higher student achievement, and we're going to insist that you continue to do those things. We've found some other requirements where the evidence is ambiguous, so we'll leave the compliance with those requirements up to you. And we've found some requirements that are inversely—perhaps I should say *perversely*—related to student achievement, so I'd like you to stop doing those right away."

This need not be a fantasy. You will read about educational leaders who have accomplished long-term sustained improvements in student achievement and educational equity and who have reduced their strategic plans to a single page. This is terrible news for consultants who are paid by the ream of paper that they produce, but it is great news for busy school leaders.

6

Leadership Leverage: Focusing on Changes with the Greatest Results

School leaders are often held accountable for things beyond their control. The skills that students bring to kindergarten; the educational attainment of families in the community; the local tax base; the pool of available teacher candidates—all these factors affect student achievement. Because complaining about things outside our control is a demonstrably ineffective leadership strategy, it is more productive to focus on the key factors that we can directly influence, including these: teacher assignment, professional development, collaboration, time, and meetings.

Teacher Assignment

The most important resource any education leader allocates is teachers. Ask yourself this question: "Does every student in my school have an equal opportunity to receive an education from the best teachers and take the most advanced courses that we can offer?" The all-too-typical answer is that the least experienced and least qualified teachers are assigned to the classes with the most complex and challenging student needs, whereas the teachers with the most experience and highest qualifications teach the most motivated and self-directed students. In a recent study, Yun and Moreno (2006) suggest that this problem is pervasive, with schools whose student populations are dominated by African American and Hispanic students significantly less likely to have certified teachers and access to advanced classes than schools where white and Asian students dominate the student population. It doesn't have to be that way.

Consider the example of Whittier Union High School District in California. The district has more than 13,500 high school students, more than 80 percent of whom are Latino and a large percentage of whom are economically disadvantaged. Superintendent Sandy Thorstenson has seen the percentage of students passing the state math exam rise from 37 percent in 2001 to 79 percent in 2006. It is no accident that many senior teacher-leaders agreed to take on the challenge of struggling math students.

In most cases, principals and department heads have the authority to ensure that teacher and course assignments are equitable. But in some districts, collective bargaining agreements limit the ability of leaders to change course assignments of teachers. Thus the most experienced teachers can choose to work with the most advantaged students, and the least experienced teachers—including many who are not qualified to teach the classes to which they are assigned—dominate the faculties of struggling schools.

Even in these situations, however, leaders can use creative options to improve the equitable distribution of teachers. Even when bargaining agreements prevent leaders from offering financial incentives to teachers who take on challenging classes in disadvantaged schools, creative leaders can offer nonfinancial incentives. For example, principals should consider offering teachers in the toughest classes lower class sizes, more planning time, more professional development opportunities, and greater levels of self-direction. More important, leaders must attend to every teacher's basic needs, such as personal safety and professional respect. Without them, even the most creative financial and nonfinancial incentives will not attract teachers to challenging teaching environments.

Professional Development

Leaders set the direction of the professional development agenda. Unfortunately, some schools are still influenced by vendors who cram every available second of professional development time with mind-numbing workshops. Ironically, we may find 500 teachers in a dark auditorium listening to an expert lecture at length about the need for differentiated instruction—*in precisely the same way to each teacher*. If your school is stuck in this model of professional development, consider focusing on a few things: what to teach, how to teach it, how to meet the needs of individual students, and how to build internal capacity. With an emphasis on internal capacity, the leadership of professional development efforts comes from the faculty itself, and a large part of professional education takes places in the classroom while teachers are engaged in authentic teaching. For example, at Ocean View Elementary School in Norfolk, Virginia, principal Lauren Campsen and a team of grade-level leaders provide professional development opportunities throughout the year, including coaching, model lessons, and data analysis. Teachers learn about differentiated instruction through hands-on differentiated professional development. Half of Ocean View's students are eligible for free or reduced-price lunch, and 62 percent of the students are ethnic minorities. In 2001, 53 percent of students were proficient in reading, and in 2006, more than 90 percent of students met that standard.

Collaboration

Imagine a football game in which each referee had a different opinion about the shape of the ball, the dimensions of the field, and the height of the goalposts. In the event of such a calamity, all the spectators would rise and yell, "That's not fair!" Yet the same scenario plays out every day in English, science, social studies, and mathematics classes, as teachers interpret "proficiency" in their own way.

Because fairness is as important inside the classroom as on the athletic field, effective leaders allocate faculty time to collaboration. In Roland Barth's (1990) dichotomy, this term does not imply just *congeniality*, but also *collegiality*. The former is about getting along in the tradition of hot coffee, good bagels, and little professional challenge; the latter is about the tough work of examining real student needs. After all, if the adults cannot agree on what proficiency means, then how are students supposed to figure it out?

In Bristol, Connecticut, former superintendent Mike Wasta and current superintendent Philip Streifer have made collaborative scoring part of the ethic of the school system's improvement efforts in the past several years. Rather than traditional faculty meetings, teachers and administrators collaboratively score real examples of student work. When they disagree, they work out their disagreements, clarify the scoring guides, and as a result improve the clarity of the assignments.

In Wayne Township, Indiana, superintendent Terry Thompson knows that teachers may not always agree on scoring student assignments. But he has some schools post on their data boards the percentage of teacher agreement on collaborative scoring exercises. If the percentage falls below 80 percent, then the faculty knows that they must work on the clarity and consistency of their scoring.

Time

Principals and superintendents can exert considerable influence over the allocation of time within the school day. For example, schools that devote an exceptional amount of time to literacy—three hours a day in elementary school and double periods in middle and high school—not only perform better in English language arts but also show improved performance in science, social studies, and mathematics (Reeves, 2004a). Of course, any change in the schedule involves trade-offs— when more time is devoted to literacy, fewer hours are available for other subjects. It is not necessary to engage in every subject every day. Some schools alternate science and social studies, providing an extra period for literacy. This requires the use of "power standards" (Ains-worth, 2003) and the deliberate decision to focus on only the most essential parts of the social studies and science curriculums rather than frantically covering every chapter under the illusion that coverage is equivalent to learning. In addition, explicit literacy instruction can be effectively included in wonderfully engaging ways in music, art, physical education, science, technology, and social studies classes.

Whatever the solution to challenges in scheduling, effective leaders must provide more time during the school day. Asking teachers to "work smarter" without giving them more time is not a sufficient solution when students are several years behind in reading. In addition, after-school and summer school programs may be part of the solution, but they alone are not sufficient to meet the needs of students who are lagging behind in literacy. This is particularly true when students most in need are least likely to participate in after-school and summer school programs.

Meetings

Principals and superintendents control meetings, which have an enormous influence on the way time is used. The same people who complain about a lack of time sometimes waste hundreds of person-hours reading announcements and tolerating political agendas. Instead, they could say, "Good morning, ladies and gentlemen. I have provided our usual administrative announcements in e-mail and written form, so we will devote the rest of our meeting to the following learning activity . . . ," thus putting themselves literally and figuratively on the same side of the table as the faculty. Faculty meetings, formerly dominated by dull announcements and endless discussions, would then focus on student learning, creative teaching strategies, collaborative scoring, and the development of engaging assessments and individualized instruction.

7

The Right Team: Selecting Teachers and Administrators

Of all the variables that influence student achievement, the two that have the most profound influence are teacher quality and leadership quality. Linda Darling-Hammond (Darling-Hammond & Sykes, 1999) has been the foremost advocate of the effect of teacher quality on student achievement, and similar conclusions have been reached by Yun and Moreno (2006), Haycock (1998), and many others. The effect of leadership on student achievement was documented extensively by Goodlad (1994) and more recently by Davis, Darling-Hammond, LaPointe, and Meyerson (2005) and by Leithwood, Louis, Anderson, and Wahlstrom (2004).

The practical question is this: How do we use this research to make better selections of teachers and principals? School leaders are frustrated with the limitations of interviews. After all, more than 90 percent of interviewees claim that they "like people" (Buckingham, 2007), even though our personal experience shows that such a high percentage is an exaggeration. Moreover, as Buckingham explains, most candidates magically transform their weaknesses into strengths. The first candidate admits reluctantly, "I guess I am a bit of a perfectionist," while the competing candidate's weakness is a tendency to work too hard. How could any superintendent or principal resist candidates with such alluring weaknesses?

My recent fieldwork has revealed three promising practices that help schools move from interview hype to practical reality. These practices are classroom observations, data analysis, and reviews of student work.

Classroom Observations

Carla Santorno, chief academic officer of the Seattle Public Schools, provided a brilliant example of performance assessment for adults when she arranged for all principal candidates to observe several different classrooms and then invited the prospective leaders to tell her what they saw. These direct observations allow for multiple levels of analysis, from the objective (Did the candidate notice important characteristics of instruction and classroom environment?) to the subtle (Did the candidate appear to enjoy being around students?).

When leadership candidates must spend time around real students and in authentic classroom environments, the realism of school trumps the contrivance of the sterile interview environment. "I like people" yields to the painful observation that some candidates just do not seem to be very comfortable around kids. Moreover, if the interviewers will be patient, they can learn a great deal about the candidate's views about the antecedents of student learning. Rather than ask, "Did you notice Mr. McRae's open-ended questioning?" the wise interviewers will simply ask, "What did you notice? What do you think?" Inevitably, the conversation will take one of two turns. The candidate may talk about instructional practices, the classroom environment, and the variables that teachers and leaders can control. On the other hand, the candidate may simply notice the characteristics of the students. With the best intentions and most sympathetic affect, the candidate might say, "The children in this school really need our understanding, and they are doing the best they can." Although such a statement sounds like an expression of empathy, it must be further tested by the second interview technique, data analysis.

Data Analysis

One midwestern superintendent invites every candidate for teacher and principal positions to interviews an hour before the scheduled time. He then provides data on two different classrooms—one high-performing and one low-performing—with a rich array of data on student achievement and demographic characteristics. What this thoughtful superintendent is looking for is the analysis of achievement. Most candidates will start the conversation by saying, "Well, the first school must be a Title I school," or "I want you to know that I understand that the first school has so many second-language students and ethnic minorities, there must be extraordinary challenges here." Only a few candidates will look deeply into the data and guide the conversation about instructional practices, pursuing questions about differences in instruction, curriculum, and assessment in the schools represented by the two data sets.

The superintendent who wishes to hire teachers and principals committed to equity is interested in listening to only those candidates who focus on teaching and leadership practices. Every interviewee will dutifully chant "All children can learn" and swear that they believe in equity. But when confronted with different data sets, only a few focus their attention on the actions of teachers and school leaders rather than the demographic characteristics of students.

Reviews of Student Work

Thoughtful researchers have long extolled the virtues of looking at real student work (Mitchell, 1996). At the very least, every person being interviewed as a teacher or a principal should be given anonymous pieces of student work and asked to evaluate that work compared to the school, district, state, provincial, or national standard for academic quality. This is analogous to a restaurant inspector being expected to look at hygiene factors in a sample kitchen and then being asked to render an accurate judgment. It is a modest performance assessment that is, incredibly, absent in most teacher and principal interviews.

But the best interviewers will not stop there. New research by economists Steven Levitt and Stephen Dubner (2006) suggests that our analysis of people and their work is colored, to use precisely the correct term, by our perception of the ethnicity of the student whose work we are evaluating. If you want to find teachers and principals who not only love and care about children, but also love them enough to tell them the truth, give them feedback, and expect them to improve their performance regardless of their predispositions, then try this provocative interview technique. Give the interview candidates samples of student work—all from the same anonymous student but associated with fictitious student names such as James Reeves, Shaneequa Coleman, Jennifer Chen, and George Martinez. Ask the candidates to grade the work and make narrative comments about each piece of work. If the work is all from the same anonymous student, you might expect to see comparable ratings for all four pieces of work. But the likelihood of that similarity is very low. Some candidates may, as Levitt and Dubner's research suggests, attribute low ratings to the candidates that they perceive to be from African American or Latino backgrounds, just as some landlords attribute less desirable characteristics to prospective tenants from the same backgrounds. Call this the "attribution error," well known to every African American school leader or business executive who has been guilty of "driving while black."

But there is a different error to which those interviewing teachers and school leaders must be sensitive. This error occurs when candidates for teaching and school leadership positions offer opposite, but no less harmful, evidence of stereotypes. As they look at student work that would not be regarded as acceptable from James or Jennifer, the prospective teacher might strive mightily to find virtue in the same work submitted by Shaneequa or George. Call this the "sympathy error." The "sympathy error" is not better than the "attribution error"; it is rather the same problematic thinking dressed up in different clothing. Although students clearly are not served well by bigots who engage in the attribution error, they also are poorly served by teachers and leaders who supplant sympathy for honest feedback.

Only a performance assessment—classroom reviews, data analyses, and a consideration of authentic student work—will transform interviews from sterile exercises in exchanging code words into a thoughtful analysis of attitudes, beliefs, and professional practices.

8

Building Capacity with Coaching

Remember when the coach was the person on the sidelines during an athletic event using a combination of encouragement, commands, and wild gestures to exhort the team on to victory? Now the proliferation of instructional coaches, leadership coaches, and life coaches has made the term *coaching* more popular but less precise. In this chapter, we explore recent research on coaching and provide some practical advice on mistakes to avoid and opportunities to get the most from a coaching relationship.

What is coaching and who does it? The answers vary widely. The Harvard Business School model (Luecke, 2004) suggests that managers and supervisors should use coaching strategies with their direct reports in order to improve performance and teamwork. Goldsmith and Lyons (2006), by contrast, suggest that the coaching relationship is distinct from supervision and evaluation and recommends that the role of coach be assigned to an independent person not in the direct line of supervision of the person receiving coaching.

In school systems around the United States, I have seen both models at work, including coaches who are also principals, central office administrators, and superintendents. More commonly, however, coaching in education makes use of independent practitioners, including retired administrators who coach new principals, veteran teachers who coach teachers facing significant challenges, and a broad range of consultants who provide instructional and leadership coaching.

Research on Coaching

Research supporting the effectiveness of coaching is inconsistent. Sherman and Freas's (2004) meta-analysis of coaching research in all fields since 1937 revealed only 131 peer-reviewed studies; of these, just 56 were empirical, and few met standards of reliable methodology. They comment, "Like the Wild West of yesteryear, this frontier is chaotic, largely unexplored, and fraught with risk, yet immensely promising" (p. 84). By contrast, John Birch, an executive coach in New Britain, Connecticut, cites multiple private studies, including those from the Manchester Consulting Company, Right Management Consultants, and Booz, Allen, and Hamilton, that boast of spectacular results (personal communication, August 20, 2007). Birch's collection of studies, based on interviews with hundreds of managers, claimed that coaching results in improved productivity, better relationships with direct reports and supervisors, improved teamwork, and greater job satisfaction. How do we sort out the conflicting claims about coaching? The best place to start is with greater precision in defining what coaching is—and what it is not—in the context of schools and educational systems.

Two Coaching Models

Two differing definitions of the coach's role seem to predominate in the literature. In one version, the coach is a cross between a bar-stool buddy and a therapist—a person with whom you can blow off steam and a trusted ally who will give you support when the world around you seems hypercritical. The focus of this coaching role is on the short-term emotional needs of the leader rather than the performance needs of the school or the district. This coaching role may serve neither need well. Coaches are rarely licensed therapists, and leaders who are suffering from stress and anxiety may need a therapeutic intervention, perhaps including appropriate medical care. When coaching attempts to meet that need, it can be counterproductive, causing leaders to delay getting the help that they need.

The second version of coaching focuses exclusively on individual and organizational performance. With a clear protocol that considers the evidence of current practice and results compared with the necessary results, performance coaching includes a focused exploration of a learning agenda, experimentation with new leadership strategies, feedback on effectiveness, and a relentless comparison of the present to the ideal state (Boyatzis & McKee, 2005).

One principal in Nevada (who preferred that I not use her name) faced exceptional challenges in a chronically underperforming school. She needed practical advice on making immediate changes in schedule, student interventions, and faculty support. With the guidance of her coach, she created flexibility in the schedule to provide literacy intervention, made long overdue changes in teaching assignments by providing strong teachers to students with the greatest needs, and communicated clearly and consistently to her supervisor from the district office. As is the case in many large school systems, a single supervisor was responsible for more than 20 schools in this district, and therefore most central office supervisors were focused on crises and correcting mistakes. The coach for this principal, in contrast, was consistently available with support and practical guidance.

When Is Coaching Useful?

Effective coaching focuses on changing performance. Therefore, the first requirement of any coaching relationship is that the person receiving the coaching must agree that a change in performance will be useful. Throwing coaches at teachers and principals who have not first agreed that improved student performance is essential will be a waste of time and money.

The second prerequisite of effective coaching is the creation of a learning and performance agenda. Educators and administrators have typically received thousands of hours of formal education and professional development. But there remains an enormous "knowing-doing" gap (Pfeffer & Sutton, 2000) that will not be bridged by yet another seminar, book, or speech. Only with a clear commitment to link learning with individual performance can a coaching relationship succeed.

The third requirement for successful coaching is feedback that is specific, accurate, and timely. Goleman, Boyatzis, and McKee (2002) make clear that feedback of this sort is the missing element in most leadership encounters, and my own research in principal and superintendent evaluations (Reeves, 2004c) confirms that the lack of specific, accurate, and timely feedback also plagues educational leaders.

Who Is Qualified to Coach?

My personal online search for organizations that train coaches revealed about 120. Almost all of these are oriented toward business and "life" coaching, although several are focused specifically on instructional and leadership coaching for education. Nevertheless, just as an advanced degree alone is no guarantee of intellectual ability or teaching competence, a certification alone is an insufficient basis on which to engage a leadership coach.

Ideally, the selection of the coach is a mutual decision of the school system and the person who will receive the coaching. The interpersonal skills and professional background of the prospective coach will influence the extent to which the coaching relationship will be successful. The selection of a coach is therefore a function of how the prospective coach will respond to the following critical questions.

Who is the client? If the prospective coach insists that the person, rather than the school or district, is the coach's only client, then it is a red flag that the personal self-esteem of the teacher or leader, not their performance, will be the focus of the coaching relationship. As the meta-analysis indicated, that helps neither the leader nor the organization.

What are the rules on confidentiality? The coaching literature reveals a sharp division about the confidentiality of coaching relationships, with the majority of sources I have read insisting upon confidentiality. However, in the context of schools, some state laws explicitly limit confidentiality agreements when the safety of students is at stake. Although those laws typically are limited to situations involving reports of child abuse, the knowledge the coach has may create a moral obligation to the organization that transcends the bounds of confidentiality. The coach may learn that someone in the organization has a substance abuse problem or that the leader being coached is impaired. If there is a chance that those people might be behind the wheel of a vehicle with students or other employees, then the coach's promises of confidentiality become secondary to the obligation to the client for student and staff safety. The same holds true when a coach becomes aware of behavior such as harassment that may expose the organization to liability. The coach is neither clergy nor therapist, but is a professional engaged to improve individual and organizational performance.

When will we know that we are successful? Successful coaching relationships are based on explicit targets and ideally include a balance of results and personal performance indicators. For example, although it is tempting for the leader to say, "We'll be successful when we improve student achievement," that is only part of the equation. After all, it's relatively easy to increase average test scores if we accept a higher dropout rate. Broader performance indicators might include not only organizational performance but also specific leadership skills, such as confronting performance issues among subordinates, improving staff relationships in specific and measurable ways, and creating improved time management and personal health disciplines. Performance goals must be specific and measurable, with the definition of success agreed upon by district and school leadership.

When will we know that the coaching relationship can be concluded? Here the coaching profession can take a cue from the best therapists, who do not seek permanent relationships with patients but rather are engaged to address specific issues and work toward a specific resolution of them. When coaching (or therapy) goes on for years without a planned conclusion to the relationship, it is a sign of aimlessness and potential dependency, not the achievement of explicit performance goals.

A Cautionary Note

Despite the enormous popularity of coaching, the jury is out on whether this development has been a good use of time and resources. Research on coaching from other fields (Boyatzis & McKee, 2005; Goleman et al., 2002) clearly indicates that only very specific types of coaching with a performance orientation will be linked to improved results. Until more education coaching meets that research-based standard, let the buyer beware.

9

Making Strategic Planning Work

The term *strategic planning* brings to mind for some people a disciplined and thoughtful process that links the values, mission, and goals of a school system with a set of coherent strategies and tasks designed to achieve those goals. For others, *strategic planning* induces a cringe brought about by memories of endless meetings, fact-free debates, three-ring binders, and dozens—perhaps hundreds—of discrete objectives, tasks, strategies, plans, and goals, all left undone after the plan was completed. As one frustrated administrator said to me, "When do we get to stop planning and start doing?"

Advocates of strategy (Cook, 2004; Porter, 1980) suggest that strategic planning is essential in any complex endeavor. This need is illustrated by an exchange between Alice and the Cheshire Cat in Lewis Carroll's (1898) *Alice's Adventures in Wonderland*. Alice begins,

> "Would you tell me, please, which way I ought to go from here?"
> "That depends a good deal on where you want to get to," said the Cat.
> "I don't much care where—" said Alice.
> "Then it doesn't matter which way you go," said the Cat. (p. 64)

Typical quotations of this exchange end here. But a more complete reading of Charles Dodgson, the math teacher who wrote under the name Lewis Carroll, reveals a nuance that is directly linked to the Law of Initiative Fatigue. Carroll's ridiculous characters give us a clear warning through parody: don't stop to analyze the data; just trudge onward. Let's pick up the dialogue between Alice and the Cheshire Cat where we left it:

> "Then it doesn't matter which way you go," said the Cat.
> "—so long as I get *somewhere*," Alice added as an explanation.
> "Oh, you're sure to do that," said the Cat, "if you only walk long enough." (pp. 64–65)

The real lesson from the little-known math instructor is a warning not only against the absence of a plan but also against the perils of excessive confidence in one's own hard work as a substitute for vision. School leaders around the globe work hard, as confident as Alice that they will get *somewhere*. They march valiantly past the Cheshire Cat colleagues and stakeholders who have seen the limits of hubris many times in the past. Leaders must, Dodgson makes clear, possess not only earnestness and energy but also clarity and focus. Otherwise, our most prodigious energies will follow Alice down the proverbial rabbit hole.

This chapter considers both advocates and critics of strategic planning and suggests some principles that can guide educational leaders in that process. I also share some promising research on the specific elements of school and district planning that are most linked to improvements in student achievement.

Strategery—When Planning Goes Wrong

Schmoker (2004) notes how many strategic planning processes that were designed to impel a district to action can have the opposite effect, substituting the development of long-term vision, mission, and goals for the imperatives of daily action to improve student results:

> We wound up setting an impossible number of "goals," even as the word was used almost interchangeably with "action steps" or "objectives." Even the "evaluation" or "results" columns were often indistinguishable from the "goals" and "action steps"—as mere implementation or training was used as evidence of having met a goal. Nonetheless, these annual plans, like the hundreds I've seen since then, were approved pro forma. There was real fear of criticizing their content and so alienating any of the numerous constituents who had spent their valuable time producing them. Instructional quality—and levels of achievement—were typically unaffected by any of these processes. (p. 426)

Kotter (2007) suggests that education is hardly unique in failing to transform strategy into action, concluding that more than 70 percent of business strategic plans are never implemented. Cartoonist Scott Adams has ridiculed the mission, vision, and strategic planning process when, appearing to be a strategy consultant, he helped groups of leaders to create ponderous and banal mission statements until the earnest participants learned that they were part of a ruse by the creator of Dilbert. Indeed, the "mission statement generator" that once resided at www.Dilbert.com could create some eerily realistic mission statements by stringing together consultant jargon. Even *Saturday Night Live* got into the act with the malapropism "strategery." Somewhere between self-important navel gazing and unremitting ridicule we should be able to find some practical guidance for school leaders who want to have rational planning processes but who want the plans to lead to improved student results.

Elements of Effective Planning

In a recent analysis of hundreds of plans from schools, central office departments, and entire districts, Stephen White (2005) and I (Reeves, 2006b) outlined some practical suggestions to get more out of the planning process. First, we analyzed the plans using a double-blind scoring rubric; that is, each plan was reviewed by at least two independent raters and scored on between 15 and 20 different dimensions of planning, implementation, and monitoring (PIM). If the two scorers failed to agree more than 80 percent of the time, they started the process again until they achieved consistent ratings. We then compared the elements of the plan ratings to student achievement in a baseline year, and then to gains in student achievement in the next year. The findings were striking: even after controlling for demographic variables of the schools, schools with higher PIM scores had higher student achievement and significantly greater gains in student achievement.

These findings, however, are hardly an endorsement of the creation of school and district plans. Every participant in the study had a plan, but only some particular types of plans were associated with improved achievement. Specifically, schools with plans that had the highest scores in monitoring, evaluation, and inquiry experienced two to five times the gains as schools that had similar plans but low scores on those three dimensions.

High scores on monitoring are awarded to schools in which there is a consistent and frequent (at least monthly) analysis of student performance, teaching strategies, and leadership practices, whereas low scores on monitoring are associated with schools that engage in the futile exercise of the educational autopsy—an analysis of last year's scores long after it is too late to do anything about them.

High scores on evaluation are awarded to schools in which every program, initiative, and strategy is subject to the relentless question "Is it working?" Whereas low-scoring schools settle for descriptions in the passive voice ("teachers were trained"), schools with high scores on evaluation are learning systems in which faculty members challenge themselves to find the relationship between their professional practices and changes in student achievement. The distinctive characteristic of schools with superior evaluation systems is that their leaders can identify practices that they have *stopped doing* as a result of insufficient evidence of effectiveness.

Schools that excel in the "inquiry" variable are those that attribute the cause of student achievement to teachers and leaders rather than to student demographic characteristics. This variable is reminiscent of the "Pygmalion effect" (Rosenthal & Jacobson, 1968), which was demonstrated when teachers were told that their students were either fast or slow learners, although in fact there was little difference among the student groups. Within a single school year, students lived up to—and down to—teacher expectations, rendering the relationship between teacher belief systems and student achievement a self-fulfilling prophecy. Similarly, schools whose plans reflect a confidence in teaching and leadership as the cause of student achievement have had achievement gains three times greater than schools whose plans reflect a focus on student demographic characteristics as the primary causes of student achievement (Reeves, 2008). This new evidence suggests that the Pygmalion effect is as strong among adults as it was 40 years ago between adults and students.

One-Page Plans

Einstein warned that we should seek to make things as simple as possible, but not more so. Therefore, the replacement of piles of three-ring strategic-planning binders with slogans is hardly a productive step.

However, there is evidence that schools are well served by one-page plans that are clearly focused and sufficiently simple so that all participants in the process understand their role in executing the plan.

Joe Crawford, former assistant superintendent for curriculum and instruction in Freeport, Illinois, reports significant gains in achievement and reductions in equity gaps during the more than five years in which each school and the district as a whole have used one-page plans (personal interview, October 5, 2007). The percentage of students who met or exceeded state standards in reading and math increased for both majority and minority students by more than 30 percent over five years. Crawford's "plan on a page" identifies four key areas: student performance, human resources, partnerships, and equity. For each of these key areas, the plan lists between two and five goals and measures. For each goal, there is a clear statement of actions to be accomplished. For example, here is one of the district's 2007–2008 goals for student performance: "By June 2008, 87 percent of the students will meet or exceed [reading standards] and 92 percent will meet or exceed [math standards]." Here is the associated action plan: "By August 31, 2007, each school will identify students below grade level on state exams and/or local assessments to receive additional support to move students to grade level." (See Appendix B for Freeport's "Plan on a Page" for 2007–2008.)

The transition from traditional plans to the plan on a page was not easy, Crawford reports. But Superintendent Peter Flynn built partnerships with the community and businesses, including the Freeport African-American Ministers United for Change. This group was a powerful advocate for developing new strategies to close the equity gap. There was broad dissatisfaction with traditional planning processes that consumed paper, time, and resources but did not lead to improved results. In addition to brevity, the new planning practices focused not only on test scores but also on measurable adult actions and on quarterly performance updates for students and adults throughout the year.

Strategy Without Strategic Plans

Contrast these two definitions of strategy. On one hand, Kotter (2007) offers simplicity itself: strategy is a collection of actions that add value. Cook (2004), on the other hand, purports the following:

> Strategic planning remains today as simple as it was 5,500 years ago: it is *the means by which those of one accord continuously create artifactual* [sic] *systems to serve extraordinary purpose*. All that is required is strategic organization, dealing with strategic issues, making strategic decisions, and taking strategic action. (p. 75)

In the end, school leaders must decide if the essential purpose of planning is to develop a tool to improve student achievement—actions that add value—or if the planning process is an end in itself. School leaders can, in brief, embrace strategy with plans that are focused and brief and that provide consistent monitoring and evaluation. Most important, effective strategies are executed by teachers and leaders who begin the process with the confidence that their professional practices influence student achievement.

PART 3

Implementing Change

The "knowing-doing" gap persisted in organizations long before Pfeffer and Sutton (2000) popularized the term. Our ancient ancestors might have enjoyed heated schools and comfortable buses much earlier had there not been such visceral opposition to the new initiatives of fire and the wheel. Do you think I am exaggerating? In his analysis of changes that profoundly influenced the course of history, Jared Diamond (1999) makes the compelling case that a few small changes in some societies—some leading to progress and others leading to disaster—had effects with consequences that lasted for centuries. In fact, when those changes led to the extinction of cultures, peoples, and species, the effect of change could hardly have been more permanent.

When considering the enormous consequences of change, it is tempting to be overwhelmed by the complexity and scope of the process. In Part 3 of this book, beginning with Chapter 10, we seek to demystify the process of change, considering specific examples of success. Newly published research on closing the implementation gap, for example, suggests that we must redefine in a radical new way the concept of "critical mass." We know what has not worked: the traditional practice of a change initiative led by the enthusiastic 3 percent who attend a conference and return to their school full of missionary zeal and, if they are enormously persuasive, double their effect—to 6 percent of the faculty. A year later, with 94 percent of their colleagues disengaged from the process, they conclude, "Well, it seems that change initiative didn't work," and they seek another inspiring conference from which they can launch the same ineffectual cycle.

Sometimes it's not as bad as that—it's worse. The leader might conclude that the original 3 percent were not the right people on whom to base the new initiative, so a different set of initiative leaders is selected, and thus begins not just a new cycle but a different cycle, with a different 3 percent. Ultimately, the organization is fraught with strife, with factions of 3 to 6 percent of the faculty all arguing over what the received wisdom should be.

The new research contrasts faculties that implemented the *same change initiatives* and claimed the *same initiative labels* but had vastly different levels of implementation. The results are striking: when 90 percent or more of a faculty was actively engaged in the change initiative, student achievement results in reading, science, and math were dramatically higher than when the same initiative was introduced with only 10 percent of the faculty actively engaged. Therefore, the variable is not simply the program, the label, the guru, or the conference. The variable is *implementation*.

In Part 2, we addressed the challenge of goal proliferation, in which the planning process undermines effective implementation because having too many goals destroys implementation before it starts. In Part 3, we provide compelling examples of schools that have taken up the challenge and, with remarkable focus and commitment, have gained widespread implementation. Note well: they did not always gain widespread "buy-in"—in fact, they faced active opposition, as described in Chapter 11. The lesson here is a critical one. Leaders do not gain buy-in through inspiration, demands, pleading, or seminars. They gain buy-in through *getting results that demonstrate that the effect*

of the change is in the best interests of all stakeholders. This section provides examples of improvements in grading, teaching, and leadership
practices that, when they were proposed, encountered significant opposition. The leaders did not give vague assurances of success and carefully worded caveats that "after all, change takes a long time." Rather,
they provided measureable, clear, and significant results in one or two
semesters. If you can deliver a change that will reduce suspensions and
discipline, reduce failure and dropouts, increase student engagement,
and improve faculty morale—all in one year or less—then you don't
wait for "buy-in," but rather you make the change and use the results to
gain sustained support.

Change leaders in schools know that we are engaged not only in
the work of education but also in a complex enterprise of people, with
all the human drama that accompanies personal pride and identity.
The best change leaders use the primacy of people as a strategy, not
an obstacle. Fullan (2008) does not exaggerate when he admonishes
leaders to love their employees and engage them at every level. In
the school context, this is unlikely to happen when the "systemwide
change initiative" is reflected only in reading and math scores. Chapter 12 makes the case that educational leaders must stop the false
dichotomy between academic and "nonacademic" classes—as if the
latter even existed in a school worthy of its mission. When music and
art (and, we could add, world languages, physical education, technology, and every other class) are recognized for their academic value and
their potential for student engagement, then we have a much greater
possibility of nurturing and sustaining learning communities.

Finally, we explore the need for descriptive rigor in any change
effort. Related research from more than 100 schools offers a scary challenge to every leader: Do your colleagues really know what you expect?
For example, when the question is "What is good reading instruction?"
the most honest answer is "Despite all of the hours, dollars, memos,

and exhortations of the past years for this ultimate priority, we really don't know." Try the same experiment with your colleagues, asking them to write on a blank piece of paper their response to this question: "What are the five most important elements of good reading instruction?" Collect the responses and evaluate for yourself how consistent they are. No matter how many "walk-throughs" and other observations leaders conduct, the exercise will be futile if those being observed are earnestly working at activities that the leader is not looking for. If your change initiatives include the basics of reading instruction, Chapter 13 deserves careful consideration. If your change initiatives are more complex and challenging than primary reading instruction, then this chapter deserves even greater consideration.

Select the initiative—equity, quality, service, achievement, engagement (the list is a long one)—and try the same experiment. Ask people to write on a blank piece of paper their response to the question "What do these terms mean?" and see if you get the same answer from everyone. If you don't, the problem is not with your colleagues. After all, if a leader noticed that almost every student at every performance level was misunderstanding an important concept in a class, the leader would not conclude that all of the children suffered from a deep flaw limited to that particular learning expectation. Rather, the leader would examine the curriculum, the teaching, the students' prior knowledge, and the feedback systems to learn how the adults could improve their practices in order to help the students become more successful. Similarly, when almost every faculty member has a divergent view of what a prospective change initiative really means, the problem is not with the faculty. Rather, the work of effective change implementation requires considerably more clarity and consistency from the leader.

10

Closing the Implementation Gap

Domino's Pizza estimates that it delivered more than 1.2 million pizzas on Superbowl Sunday. I estimate that more than a million of those pies were delivered to people like me, who had, only a few weeks earlier, resolved to give up pizza, as well as the beer and chips we consumed while watching the game.

If our annual tradition of leaving our New Year's goals in tatters has any redeeming value, it's the lesson about the foolishness of believing that creating a list of goals is enough. Just as New Year's resolutions rarely survive until February, many promising school plans never break out of the confines of three-ring binders. We have the goals and the plans. The challenge is closing the implementation gap.

Good News, Bad News

The good news about closing the implementation gap is that we know what to do. Education research has equipped us with abundant evidence on instructional and leadership strategies that are likely to result in improved student achievement (Marzano, Waters, & McNulty, 2005; White, 2005).

Evidence, however, is strikingly powerless against the drivers of human behavior. Despite medical research establishing the association between cigarette smoking and lung cancer, educated people, including physicians, still smoke. The same people who would never buy a washing machine without consulting *Consumer Reports* sometimes use risky, untested medications in response to late-night television testimonials. And yes, teachers and school leaders persist in using ineffective teaching strategies, toxic grading policies, and counterproductive leadership tactics despite an avalanche of evidence that suggests better alternatives. The challenge before us is not a shortage of evidence or a lack of goals, but our collective failure to take the difficult step of implementing strategies to reach those goals.

Every organization—indeed, every person—suffers to some degree from a gap between intention and action. Leadership can make the difference. Here are a few specific strategies that can bring implementation closer to reality.

Implementation Strategies

Create short-term wins. Psychologist Martha Beck (2006) marshals impressive evidence that individuals need immediate, continuing reinforcement to sustain meaningful changes. Tom Peters (2003) makes the same case for organizational change. Too many school initiatives provide their chief feedback through annual test score reports—results that are almost never delivered until it's too late to reinforce or modify teachers' or leaders' behavior.

Effective leaders design plans in the spring and summer that will produce short-term wins within the first few weeks of school. For example, every two weeks principals can post the percentage of the faculty that agreed on the score of a collaboratively evaluated student assignment. The higher the percentage, the more effective the collaboration and the clearer the scoring guide. This is particularly important when the faculty has experienced turnover during the summer, and, unintentionally, they are sending very different signals to students about their expectations. Counselors can post behavioral data, signaling that as expectations are more clearly and consistently communicated during the early days of the semester, the student climate improves. Faculty members can post visible evidence of interdisciplinary assignments and the resulting student work, showing colleagues and students a commitment to professional collaboration.

Formative assessment is one important way to provide short-term wins throughout the year (Ainsworth & Viegut, 2006; Popham, 2006; Stiggins, 2004). It is absolutely vital that we understand the true meaning of formative assessment—an activity designed to give meaningful feedback to students and teachers and to improve professional practices and student achievement. Tests designed only to render an evaluation cannot achieve the potential of assessment for learning that assessment experts have suggested is an essential element of effective practice.

In practice, formative assessment need not be lengthy or formal. Consider what happens in music classes every day. When a student plays a note incorrectly, the music teacher does not record the error in the grade book and inform the student's parents nine weeks later that the student needs to really work on the F-sharp. Music teachers continually assess student performance, stop when necessary to give specific feedback, and then immediately use that feedback to improve student performance. Lucy Calkins (1994) conducts writing classes for students of all ages with the same attention to formative assessment and immediate feedback.

The key to effective short-term wins is that the objectives are meaningful, are attainable, and provide immediate feedback to reinforce effective practice and modify ineffective practice. Without short-term wins, the pain of change often overwhelms the anticipated long-term benefits.

Recognize effective practices simply and clearly throughout the year. The Connecticut State Department of Education holds an annual "adult science fair"—an exposition in which professional practices and student achievement data are displayed on simple three-panel boards showing student data on the left-hand panel, adult actions on the middle panel, and inferences and conclusions on the right-hand panel. Last year, more than 200 schools contributed displays. The Stupski Foundation in San Francisco uses a similar method to identify common leadership practices among effective grant recipients and to provide a clear and highly visible accountability mechanism that also serves as a professional learning opportunity. In Clark County, Nevada, 81 teams of teachers and administrators are involved in action research projects with a commitment to transparently sharing their results. They not only display achievement scores on formative assessments but also display the professional practices associated with the scores. For example, teacher Mitchell Johnson found that during the first semester, students who made the most extensive use of Cornell note taking had scores on a national physics test that were twice as high as those who made the least use of this technique. These displays are living documents, updated to provide a regular focal point for celebrating best practices.

Emphasize effectiveness, not popularity. Too many change efforts fail because leaders have underestimated the power of the prevailing culture in undermining change. To challenge that culture, leaders must be prepared to stand up for effective practice even if changes are initially unpopular. Teachers in every school know right now which students are in danger of failure at the end of the year, and they know that with immediate intervention and extra time, many of those failures could be avoided. Yet one of the least popular actions any teacher or school leader can take is to change the schedule or curriculum of a student during the year. It is more convenient to wait for the failure at the end of the year and then attempt the same practices in the following year, all the while hoping for different results. If the litmus test for goal achievement is the short-term popularity of the changes necessary to implement the goals, then the strategy is doomed. Change inevitably represents risk, loss, and fear—a triumvirate never associated with popularity.

Make the case for change compelling, and associate it with moral imperatives rather than compliance with external authority. An announcement that "We have to do this to comply with state and federal requirements" will never arouse the emotional engagement of the school staff. Instead of citing administrative requirements, inspire staff members with a call for their best: "Student literacy is a civil right. Faculty collaboration is the foundation of fairness. Learning communities are the essence of respect."

You won't close the implementation gap with another set of three-ring binders or announcements about the latest initiative. Close the gap with immediate wins, visible recognition of what works, a focus on effectiveness rather than popularity, and a direct appeal to the values that brought us all into this profession in the first place.

11

The Flywheel: Getting Short-Term Wins to Sustain Long-Term Change

What would preventing 1,000 course failures mean for your school system? For administrators, it would mean 1,000 fewer repeated courses that have to be worked into students' schedules. For teachers, it would mean hundreds of students who are more likely to be motivated and engaged instead of angry, disengaged, and discouraged. Most important, for students, it would mean an opportunity to learn that persisting, listening to teacher feedback, and working hard really do make a difference. It would mean the chance to say with confidence, "I am a successful student."

In this chapter, we look first at the striking example of a high school in Indianapolis that has implemented a bold "no failure" campaign. Then we explore the importance of grading practices and suggest steps to take to ensure that those practices contribute to effective, long-term improvements. Finally, we consider how a new approach to attendance policies can yield significant benefits.

Strategies from an Exemplary High School

The teachers and leadership of Ben Davis High School in Indianapolis, Indiana, engaged in a "no failure" campaign in spring 2006 and reduced the number of course failures by an astounding 1,006 compared with the previous year. This comprehensive high school serving more than 3,000 students has a complex and challenging student population that includes 43 percent minority students, 9 percent English language learners, and 45 percent students who qualify for free or reduced-price lunch. Student mobility and the number of low-income and second-language students are growing. The teachers are dedicated and hardworking, but they had those characteristics long before the school achieved its dramatic reduction in student failures. What specific strategies did teachers and school leaders use to prevent 1,000 student failures? According to principal Joel McKinney, seven strategies were the key.

Early, frequent, and decisive intervention. "Every three weeks throughout the school year, teachers give us the names of students who are at risk of failure," explains McKinney. "We use this information to give students personalized assistance and avoid failures." For example, teachers, counselors, and administrators meet with students and parents as soon as there is a problem. Some students need assistance on homework, and others need help on time management and the basics of keeping an assignment notebook. Some students need assistance on basic literacy, while others need encouragement, support, and the teamwork provided by extracurricular activities. Music, art, technology, and career programs play a vital role in addressing individual student needs.

At Ben Davis, teachers do not wait until a reading problem has caused multiple course failures. They identify the reading challenge immediately. All incoming students—whether they enroll in August or at any other time during the year—receive a reading assessment. It takes less than a half hour and tells counselors immediately whether a student needs help in reading.

Personal connection with struggling students. Within weeks after the beginning of each semester, teachers at Ben Davis know which students are at risk of failure. Even in a large high school, the faculty has learned to "think small" as teachers, counselors, and administrators meet with students individually and enter into learning contracts with them. Students meet regularly with counselors and academic coaches who provide support, guidance, and, most of all, the clear signal that adults in the school care about them as individuals.

Parent connections. Rather than wait for a student's failure in a course to precipitate a parent meeting, school officials contact parents or guardians as soon as a student has been identified as being at risk for a course failure, and they schedule individual meetings to plan for additional support.

Tutoring by teachers, peer tutors, and "study buddies" provides students with one-to-one assistance. Some students thrive with computer-assisted assessment and feedback, and the district has enjoyed some success with Web-based scoring of student writing. Other students require personal connections with teachers, paraprofessionals, and peers. Computer-based grading of student papers is certainly not a replacement for personal interaction between students and teachers. But a substantial number of students find the immediate feedback provided by Vantage Learning, used in Wayne Township, and other Web-based scoring programs to be remarkably effective. It is what Dr. Jeff Howard of the Efficacy Institute has described as the "Nintendo Effect," in which students respond to feedback from electronic games because that feedback is immediate, accurate, and incremental. Students persist in playing Nintendo and other electronic games not because they receive patronizing pats on the head, but rather because they receive brutally honest feedback. When students receive a score of 2 on their electronically scored essay, they are as eager to submit a revised essay as they are to "get to the next level" when they are defeated in a Nintendo game. Teachers will never be replaced by computerized scoring, but educational leaders can leverage teachers' time by making maximum use of technology.

Managing students' choices with decisive curriculum interventions. Although educators' respect for students and parents is evident, this high school has put into place the radical notion that the adult professionals are in charge of the curriculum. Principal McKinney insists that students "can make a lot of choices, but we won't let them choose to fail." Administrators change student schedules in the middle of the semester if necessary to provide additional instruction, intervention, and assistance to students in need.

In-school assistance. Many high school students have jobs, and some live alone or in homes where parents are distracted and exhausted at the end of the day. Even when parents are deeply committed to the education of their children, the plain fact is that by the time students are in secondary school they are largely making their own choices about homework, commitment, planning, and follow-through. Therefore, Ben Davis does not rely exclusively on after-school or summer school programs for intervention for students in danger of failure; instead, the school provides daily intervention and support.

Reformed grading systems. The Ben Davis staff is well versed in the research on student feedback, grading, and motivation. Tom Guskey (2002), Tom Guskey and Jane Bailey (2001), Bob Marzano (2000), and I (Reeves, 2004a) have provided abundant evidence that grading systems are effective only if they are accurate, fair, and timely. At Ben Davis, teachers have largely eliminated the use of the zero, the inappropriate use of averages, and the assignment of poor grades as punishment.

With an understanding of student resilience, they know that it is not
how students start each semester that counts but how they finish.

Wayne Township is hardly alone in reforming its grading policies. For example, in Douglas County, Colorado, the middle school
grading policy is explicit in stating that later grades have more weight
than earlier grades. A growing number of schools differentiate between
academic proficiency and work habits because they recognize what
every teacher knows: students can be proficient in math and deficient
in work habits, and students can be delightful, compliant, and sociable,
yet deficient in math.

The literature on high school reform is full of exaggerated claims
and breathless enthusiasm for the latest silver bullet. In contrast, educators at Ben Davis—and at many other schools—are putting together
solid, comprehensive programs based on research, hard work, and the
determination that no student will slip through the cracks. As Principal McKinney notes, "It just works."

The Importance of Grading Practices

As the description of Ben Davis High School attests, changing grading systems is a key strategy for effective reform. In fact, if you wanted
to make just one change that would immediately reduce failure rates,
then the most effective place to start would be by challenging prevailing grading practices. How can I be so sure? Try this experiment at your
next faculty meeting. Ask your colleagues to calculate the final grade
for a student who receives the following 10 grades during a semester:
C, C, MA (Missing Assignment), D, C, B, MA, MA, B, A. I have done
this experiment with thousands of teachers and administrators in the
United States, Canada, Australia, and Argentina. Every time—bar

none—I get the same results: the final grade ranges from *F* to *A* and everything in between.

As this experiment demonstrates, the difference between failure and the honor roll often depends on the grading policies of the teacher. To reduce the failure rate, schools don't need a new curriculum, a new principal, new teachers, or new technology. They just need a better grading system.

Effective Versus Ineffective Grading

The results of my experiment are not surprising. Guskey and Bailey (2001) and Marzano (2000) have synthesized decades of research with similar findings. Neither the weight of scholarship nor common sense seems to have influenced grading policies in many schools. Practices vary greatly among teachers in the same school—and even worse, the practices best supported by research are rarely in evidence.

For example, we know that the most effective grading practices provide feedback that is accurate, specific, timely, and designed to improve student performance (Marzano, 2000, 2007; O'Connor, 2007). In the best classrooms, grades are only one of many types of feedback provided to students. Music teachers and athletic coaches routinely provide abundant feedback to students and only occasionally associate a grade with the feedback. Rather than evaluate the last piece of work, teachers in writing classes provide meaningful feedback on a student's expression and coherence, with the feedback designed to improve successive drafts. Teachers in visual arts, drafting, culinary arts, or computer programming allow students to create a portfolio to show their best work, knowing that the mistakes made during the course of the semester were not failures but lessons learned on the way to success. In all of these cases, each "failure" is not an *F* but a lesson learned, and it is never averaged into a calculation of the final grade at the end of the semester.

Contrast these effective practices with commonly used grading policies that are so ineffective that they can be labeled as "toxic." The first example of an ineffective policy is the use of zeroes for missing work. Despite evidence that grading as punishment does not work (Guskey, 2000) and the mathematical flaw in the use of the zero on a 100-point scale (Reeves, 2006a), many teachers routinely maintain this policy in the mistaken belief that it will lead to improved student performance. In the experiment mentioned earlier, in which educators presented with the same set of 10 grades calculate final grades ranging from A to F, the grades of F always are the result of assigning a zero for missing work. Defenders of the zero claim that "students need to have consequences" for flouting authority and failing to turn in work on time. They are right; students should have consequences for missing work, and the appropriate consequence is not a zero but *doing the work*.

Schools that are making dramatic reductions in the failure rate are not disregarding homework, but they are recognizing that, as my principal once told me, the word *homework* may or may not have anything to do with the word *home*. Part of an effective grading policy is having a sound and meaningful consequence for missing work, such as the requirement for students to complete work before, during, or after school; during study periods; at "quiet tables" at lunch; or in other settings. The presumption that every student goes home to an environment conducive to homework is not true in many schools.

The second example of an ineffective grading policy is the use of the average of all scores throughout the semester, a formula that presumes that the learning early in the semester is as important as the learning at the end of the semester (Marzano, 2000; O'Connor, 2007). It is worth noting that when teachers and administrators have been students in my graduate courses, they routinely insist that they should be evaluated based on their understanding at the end of the semester, not on an average of their work throughout the term.

The third example is the use of the "semester killer"—the single project, test, lab, paper, or other assignment that will make or break students. This practice puts 18 weeks of work at risk based upon a project that might, at most, have consumed four weeks of the semester.

A small but growing number of school systems are tackling the issue head-on with comprehensive plans for effective grading practices. (The policy developed by one such district, Grand Island Public Schools in Nebraska, is available at http://wikiassessments.editme.com/files/GradingandReporting/G%26R%20Guiding%20Docs.pdf.) But even in districts that have attempted to put effective grading policies in place, enforcement is often inconsistent. Grading seems to be regarded as the last frontier of individual teacher discretion. The same school leaders and community members who would be indignant if sports referees were inconsistent in their rulings continue to tolerate inconsistencies that have devastating effects on student achievement.

High-Stakes Grading

The Alliance for Excellent Education estimated that the annual cost of high school failure exceeds $330 billion ("An Economic Case," 2007). Some of these failures are no doubt caused by excessive absences and poor student performance. But, as the experiment mentioned earlier in this chapter clearly indicates, many failures are attributable to the differences in teachers' grading policies.

Do another experiment: randomly select 30 course failures from the last semester and determine the cause for failure. Two common causes are missing homework and poor performance on a single major assignment—a term paper, a lab, or a project. What would it mean to your school if you could reduce the number of failing grades resulting solely from uncompleted homework?

The stakes of grading practices are not limited to student failure. When grading policies improve, discipline and morale almost always follow. For example, as noted earlier, Ben Davis High School achieved a remarkable reduction in course failures with focused attention on improved feedback and intervention for students (Reeves, 2006a). Principal Joel McKinney recently reported that the success of this challenging urban school did not stop with reducing 9th and 10th grade failures. As of fall 2007, enrollment in advanced placement classes had increased 32 percent, suspensions had declined 67 percent, elective opportunities in music, art, and technology had increased, class cuts and tardiness had fallen significantly, teacher morale and school climate had noticeably improved—and the course failure rate had continued to decline (personal communication, December 5, 2007). When schools take steps to reduce failures, lots of good things happen.

The Steps to Take

Although changing grading systems is a challenging leadership task, the benefits are so great and the stakes are so high that it's worth doing.

First, create a sense of urgency. Identify the exact cost of inconsistent grading practices. Ask this question: how many failures could we prevent this semester if we improve our grading practices?

Second, identify teacher leaders who are already improving policies. Chances are there are already teachers in your school who have eliminated the use of the average (Guskey, 2000) and the zero on a 100-point scale (Reeves, 2004d) and created meaningful opportunities for corrective feedback other than grades (Marzano, 2000; O'Connor, 2007). Provide a forum for these teachers to share their insights with colleagues and lead the effort to develop improved policies.

Third, get the facts; gather evidence that will create a rationale for decision making. At the end of the day, your choices about teaching practice must be guided by evidence, not opinions. For example, although many people sincerely believe that giving poor grades as a punishment is effective, Guskey (2000) has marshaled 90 years of evidence to the contrary.

Fourth, reassure parents, students, and teachers that certain things will *not* change. Students will still have letter grades, transcripts, honor rolls, individualized education plans, and everything else that they have counted on as part of their grading system. What they won't have is irrational and toxic grading policies that give students widely different grades for the same work.

The benefits of effective grading practices are not limited to a reduced failure rate—although that benefit alone is sufficient to justify change. When student failures decrease, student behavior improves, faculty morale is better, resources allocated to remedial courses and course repetitions are reduced, and resources invested in electives and advanced courses increase. When was the last time a single change in your school accomplished all that?

Improving Student Attendance

To paraphrase educational philosopher Yogi Berra, "Showing up to school is 90 percent of the game; the other half is mental." Research is conclusive that attendance is strongly associated with student achievement (Johnson, 2000); a drop in attendance from 95 percent to 85 percent cuts in half the chances that students will pass state literacy tests. As a result, many schools have tough policies for unexcused absences, typically including no credit for homework or examinations that were missed and other penalties that are designed to motivate students to come to school. The problem is that these "get tough" mandates have proven to be counterproductive, and student tardiness and truancy remain a major challenge for many schools. Although teachers and school leaders may be tempted to increase penalties for truant students, research from Dennis Peterson, superintendent of Minnetonka Public Schools in Minnesota, and his colleagues suggests a better alternative: disconnecting grades from attendance.

The "Get Tough" Fallacy

Jeff Erickson, assistant principal at Minnetonka High School, expressed the logic of many school policies when he explained, "The previous attendance policy required the reduction of quarter/semester grades after three absences, and each subsequent unexcused absence thereafter. Tardiness, as well, caused a reduction of grades. The thinking went as follows: *If you don't arrive on time, I am going to dock your grade. If this assignment is one day past the due date, you won't receive any credit. If you skip on a test day, you fail the test.*" Erickson concluded, "Logically, one would think that the threat of reducing a student's grade would work. However, it didn't produce the results we desired" (personal communication, March 12, 2008).

When the district engaged in a bold policy change to disconnect unexcused absences from grades, there were widespread predictions that attendance, along with respect for authority, would plummet. What would students do if they no longer feared that grades would be used as a punishment for misbehavior?

Finding the Right Consequences

The key to Minnetonka's success was not the absence of consequences for absences and tardiness, but rather finding the *right* consequences. For example, rather than receiving a reduction in a grade or a zero for missed work, students who miss a single class can expect that their parents will receive a phone call (and, where available, an e-mail) within hours of the infraction; within 36 hours, students have a personal interview with a staff member to inquire about the absence. Further, every unexcused absence results in after-school detention. In the words of one student at the high school, "What is it? Last year I could skip and nobody cared. This year, I skip once and I'm taken to the wood-shed." To many outsiders, the disconnection of grading penalties from absences would seem to be a decreased consequence; the students have come to a different conclusion.

The Results: Improved Attendance

In Minnetonka, the student and faculty population was stable in the 2007–2008 school year, and the only major changes were the new policies for grading and attendance. Therefore, it is quite likely that changes in attendance and academic performance were not the result of a sudden influx of more well-behaved students, but rather the result of the change in the district's policy. After the new policy was adopted, unexcused absences dropped by 42 percent, the number of disciplinary referrals dropped by 64 percent, and suspensions dropped by 37 percent.

These results are strikingly consistent with the evidence from Indiana discussed earlier in this chapter. Certainly, the Indiana evidence is complex, and any honest evaluation of education research will conclude that it is a multivariate challenge—teaching, leadership, policy, and demographics all combine to influence student results. Yet while there are many variables at work in the complex equation of improving student achievement, the consistent fact is that when grading policies are improved, student achievement increases and behavior improves dramatically.

From Evidence to Policy

Grading and attendance policies are emotional issues, as dozens of people have made clear in their responses to some of my writing on the subject. These thoughtful correspondents generally express two common themes. A few share sentiments such as this: "We disconnected grading from student behavior, and it has been quite successful." The vast majority, however, express doubt, in terms such as this: "I believe that the evidence you have presented is correct, but my colleagues just won't buy into the idea of changing grading practices." Thus we have a situation in which (1) we have a pervasive challenge with student absences and failures; (2) we have evidence that present grading policies are part of the problem; and (3) we have evidence from the early 20th century to the present day that alternative grading policies can be effective.

How to deal with resistance to reform? I have concluded that the current "grading wars" are not dissimilar to equally vehement arguments in the 1950s and 1960s over corporal punishment in schools. Research suggested that corporal punishment validated the use of force and was therefore more likely to produce bullies and dropouts than compliance. Nevertheless, many people strongly believed that it was the only effective way to motivate students, with "the board" being the tool of choice in the junior high school I attended. But within a few years, corporal punishment disappeared from schools—not because the doubters accepted the research, but because courageous leaders made unpopular decisions that benefitted an entire generation of students, including every reader of this book who was never "motivated" by a board, a hand, or a whip. If the threshold for improving grading policies is "buy-in," then you will be the last to change. If you take the risk that the district leaders of Ben Davis High School and Minnetonka High School took, you will endure criticism, doubt, and second-guessing—at least until your school experiences improved attendance, achievement, and discipline.

The Essentials: Teaching, Leadership, Time, and Feedback

Educational leaders confront a bewildering array of recommendations, programs, and alternatives. We know that the least effective response is the simultaneous implementation of many different initiatives. But as bad as "initiative fatigue" may be at one extreme, the other extreme— analysis paralysis—is no better. So where do we start? What are the most important issues that educational leaders must address? Research and practicality lead to these four keys: teaching, leadership, time, and feedback. Teaching is the first and most important element of progress. Neither programs nor curricula nor assessments nor administrative mandates will replace the primacy of teaching effectiveness as the number one impact on student achievement. When schools claim that they are committed to achievement but systematically deny their most needy students their most effective teachers, then their claims of commitment are undermined by their policies.

Second, leadership matters. As important as teaching is to the improvement of student results, too many teachers operate as islands of excellence, persevering heroically against extraordinary odds. Their exceptional nature suggests that, by definition, they cannot become the norm and are therefore not a sustainable model for improvement. One of the most important tasks of leadership is to make what is extraordinary today become merely superior and brilliant tomorrow. Note that I do not suggest that we take the extraordinary and render it ordinary—that model, too, is not sustainable, as our colleagues in the classroom will not be emotionally sustained by a steady diet of "Good

morning! I'm pleased to notice how ORDINARY you are today!"
Wise leaders must identify, document, and replicate great practice,
making wonderful practice more common, without diminishing it as
commonplace.

Third, teachers require time. This is, as logicians would say, an a
priori condition. No matter how great the curriculum, program, assessment, or other intervention, when teachers lack the time to implement great ideas, then those ideas remain figments of a central office
fantasy rather than daily realities in the classroom. The research in this
book and elsewhere is clear: if we expect teachers to excel in literacy,
math, data analysis, assessment, or any other endeavor, then the
commitment of administrators to those goals is directly proportionate
to their willingness to adjust the schedule and support those commit-
ments with time.

The fourth and final essential is feedback. Marzano (2000, 2007)
reminds us that feedback can be one of the most powerful tools for
improving student results if and only if the feedback is accurate, timely,
and effective. School leaders should evaluate every teacher-student
interaction, from daily conversation to final exams to report cards as
subsets of the large umbrella of feedback. If any of those elements lack
the essential characteristics of accuracy, timeliness, and effectiveness,
then we have acquiesced in undermining one of the most important
contributions leaders and teachers can make to improve student
achievement.

These four essentials are, unfortunately, some of the most difficult
changes leaders will ever undertake. When policymakers tell me, as
they have in the week that this book goes to press, that the issues of
teaching, leadership, time, and feedback are just "too hot to handle"
and that "our staff and community are not ready for this," then I know
that these are policymakers who should simply surrender to the forces
against change. Certainly it is disingenuous for them to say, "We want

to make progress and we are committed to change" when their next words are "just as long as we don't have to make any changes regarding teaching, leadership, time, and feedback."

In sum, you can have a one-page plan that addresses these essential elements, and you can achieve the great things evidenced in schools described in this chapter. If you have a 300-page plan and three-ring binders stacked to the ceiling, but you do not make meaningful changes in teaching, leadership, time, and feedback, then futility is certain.

12

Building Stakeholder Support:
Academics and the Arts

Leaders set priorities. With multiple demands on the limited quantities of school resources and classroom time, one of the most essential jobs facing every school leader is the allocation of those finite resources in a way that will have the maximum effect on student success. For some schools, the imperative to raise test scores may lead administrators to sacrifice seemingly nonrelated subjects such as music and art in order to provide the time and resources necessary for success in literacy and math.

The debate is particularly contentious, even by the standards of acrimony in educational debates. Proponents of the trade-off note that if students lack essential literacy skills, then no amount of music or art will gain them economic opportunity and self-sufficiency. To do otherwise, they argue, would deny basic opportunities to underperforming students who frequently are poor and members of ethnic minorities. Social justice, they conclude, demands more time on academic subjects. Proponents of the arts claim with equal vigor that an educational system that provides the beauty, engagement, and enjoyment of the arts to the rich but not to the poor is profoundly unjust. When students

who arrive at school with sound reading skills are afforded a rich and
varied curriculum but students without those advantages are consigned
to endless reading and math drills, then we have only resegregated
classrooms and schools on racial and economic lines.

A False Dichotomy

Both sides make a compelling case. But the evidence suggests that
the stark choice between academic skills and the arts presents a false
dichotomy. Time in school need not be a "zero-sum game" in which
every moment dedicated to music and art represents a minute sacrificed from literacy and math. Great classes in the fine arts not only
provide rich stimulation for students but also are directly related to
improvements in academic success.

Let us first consider one thing on which educators in every field
can agree: when students are far behind in literacy and math skills,
summer school and after-school programs are not enough. Students
need more time during every regular school day, particularly for the
development of literacy skills (Reeves, 2004a). The longer we wait
to intervene effectively to meet student literacy needs, the worse the
conditions become. An 8th grade student who is not reading on grade
level has an 85 percent likelihood of remaining behind grade level in
reading throughout all of high school (Cappella & Weinstein, 2001).
Therefore, both sides of the argument should at least agree that literacy
is essential and that the sooner disadvantaged students catch up with
their more advantaged peers, the better for the students and society.
The opportunity for lifelong enjoyment of the arts is, at least to some
degree, dependent upon the opportunity to escape a life of poverty and
unemployment.

But what about evidence that the arts support literacy and math skills? Many teachers have anecdotal evidence about the development of math skills in a music class or the reinforcement of a rich and varied vocabulary through the use of vivid visual images in an art class. Petersen (2007) reviewed the progress of Thompson Elementary School in Aldine, Texas; Feaster-Edison Charter School, a K–6 school in Chula Vista, California; and the Elm City College Preparatory School, a K–8 school in New Haven, Connecticut. All of these schools had substantial numbers of students who were eligible for free or reduced-price lunch, and every student population included significant percentages of ethnic and linguistic minority students. Nevertheless, Petersen found that "these schools have all managed to achieve impressive results by using data on student performance in subjects like reading, math, and science, and yet all still manage to deliver a well-rounded curriculum that includes art, music, and physical education" (p. 42).

These examples are not isolated. Indeed, the 1999 Indiana Teacher of the Year, Larry Hurt, is an art teacher who makes extensive use of nonfiction writing in his classes. Jan Bowler is a music teacher in Massachusetts who regularly requires students to produce written reflections on their practices and performances. Both educators reflect the conviction of pediatrician Mel Levine (2002) that writing is "the largest orchestra a kid will ever conduct."

Other recent evidence suggests a direct and systematic link between art experiences and literacy performance. Kennedy (2006) described a recent study from the Guggenheim Museum that compared students who participated in the museum's art project with those who did not. "The study found that students in the program performed better in six categories of literacy and critical thinking skills—including thorough description, hypothesizing, and reasoning—than did students who were not in the program" (p. 1). Teachers all over the world can benefit from partnerships with museums through www.EchoSpace. org, a site that links teachers to projects such as the Alaska Native Heritage Center, the Peabody-Essex Museum in Salem, Massachusetts, the Bishop Museum in Hawaii, and the Mississippi Band of Choctaw Indians, to name just a few.

One of the most remarkable examples of effective integration of the arts into an academic curriculum comes from veteran teacher Maureen Copeland, who teaches Advanced Placement (AP) European History at Fort Myers High School in Lee County, Florida. Working with ethnically and economically diverse students, most of whom are sophomores rather than the seniors who traditionally take AP classes, Ms. Copeland routinely produces classes in which more than 80 percent pass the AP test and more than 30 percent achieve the maximum score of 5. The students are challenging, including many who need basic work in reading, writing, document analysis, and academic focus. The secret of her success? "Art is a hook," Ms. Copeland says. "I'll use Goya and David to show two perspectives on war, and 18th century Dutch paintings that reflect the relationship between colonialism and global trade." Tellingly, she adds, "The kids love it." The AP European History curriculum is notoriously dense, with far more to cover than is rational for a single-period, one-year class. How does Ms. Copeland find the time to cover such an intense curriculum and also to nurture a love of art among her students? "If it's important, you make the time," she explains. Her experience suggests that art is not an "extra" that can be indulged in when time permits, but rather an essential ingredient of superior academic instruction.

Despite abundant evidence on the association between the arts and student academic performance, critics are quick to note that there are many confounding variables at work—most particularly the socioeconomic status of the student. It is possible that students with extensive exposure to art and music have higher test scores not because of the art and music, but rather because those students are more likely to come from affluent families. Therefore, it is particularly important to note that the research cited in this chapter specifically refers to the value of music and art in schools where students are struggling academically and where they also experience disadvantages related to low income.

Strategies to Consider

Whatever the future of current federal laws, such as No Child Left Behind, the vast majority of schools will continue to regard annual test scores as an important measure of student progress, and educational leaders will ignore them at their peril. Moreover, opportunities for students continue to be related to test scores. The challenge before leaders is to preserve the beauty that the arts offer to every student without sacrificing the educational opportunities students need. Here are three strategies to consider.

First, call a truce. Educators of every subject are, first and foremost, teachers of children, not teachers of one particular discipline. We expect every teacher to teach honesty, self-discipline, and organization, and it is similarly reasonable to expect all teachers to regard literacy not as a diversion from their primary subject but as a useful way of helping students to think about their subject. We do not write in music and art class because music and art are unimportant, but rather because those subjects are so important they are worth thinking about. Writing is not merely a mechanical skill but a reflection of students' reasoning and thinking. Establish a norm that there is no such thing as a "nonacademic" class in school and that every subject is worthy of the thought and discipline that we associate with academic study.

Second, make it a two-way street. Although it is increasingly common to expect music and art teachers to integrate literacy into their lessons, wise teachers of history, English, science, and math know that music, art, and dance can form powerful visual, auditory, and kinesthetic associations that help students learn essential content and concepts.

Third, treat students as if they were rich. Imagine for a moment that you are the headmaster of an elite private school. Some students are behind in reading and math, yet you are committed to providing a solid arts education for every student. After all, parents who are paying $20,000 to $30,000 in annual tuition payments expect you to both provide necessary academic interventions and also deliver a rich and engaging arts curriculum. What would you do? Perhaps you would provide extra literacy instruction for all students, from those who are struggling to those who are advanced. You certainly would ensure that every student received opportunities to excel not only academically but also in the arts, technology, and athletics.

As leaders reflect on their challenging role in balancing the arts, academic requirements, and every other demand for resources and time, we should consider the provocative question: "What would we do if our students were rich?" Then we should ask, "Is there any public school student who deserves any less?"

13

Defining Change: Lessons from Literacy

Although there can be little doubt about the importance of literacy for student success at every level, educational leaders have a long way to go in reaching consensus on the implementation of effective literacy instruction. Although superintendents routinely expect principals to be "instructional leaders," that label does not mean very much if the leaders and teachers hold vague and inconsistent views on the most essential elements of effective instruction in literacy.

Years after the "reading wars," which brought vitriolic disagreement on reading instruction, a consensus has emerged on many elements. Even experts who disagree on some approaches (Allington, 2005; Calkins, 2001; Lyon & Chhabra, 2004) suggest some common elements of effective reading instruction: phonics, guided reading, independent reading, informal feedback, interim assessments, expert tutoring, extended time, and other strategies designed to create readers who not only are proficient but also acquire the "flashlight under the bedspread" joy of reading for pleasure. In addition, strong evidence suggests that effective literacy instruction includes writing (Calkins, 1994, 2001), with a particular emphasis on nonfiction writing (Reeves, 2002, 2004a). This consensus, however, is far from reality in the classrooms unless leaders ask four essential questions: What is effective literacy instruction? How will we ensure that teachers have time for effective literacy instruction? How will we help students who are struggling? How will leaders support consistent responses to the previous questions?

Consistent Labels, Inconsistent Implementation

Consider the evidence from more than 130 schools in three school systems on the West Coast, in the Midwest, and on the East Coast. All three systems claimed to have "nonnegotiable" standards for literacy instruction, including the time devoted to literacy and the methods of effective reading instruction. Responding to a questionnaire with the assurance of confidentiality and anonymity, administrators and teachers revealed a striking gap between the illusion of consistent delivery of literacy instruction and the reality of the classroom. Although all three systems claimed to have a strictly enforced 90-minute block for literacy, the daily time allocated for reading ranged from 45 minutes to more than three hours. Despite a claim to have immediate and mandatory intervention for struggling readers, the time provided for additional reading instruction ranged from zero to more than two hours. Most telling, when leaders and teachers were asked to identify the most important elements of effective reading instruction, the responses were not close to the consistent requirements that the district-mandated reading curriculum envisioned, with widely varying levels of emphasis on guided reading, individual work, and group work. Even when the terminology, such as "guided reading," was identical, the definition of the phrase was inconsistent.

The Teacher's Perspective

Imagine that you are a teacher attempting to do the right thing for students by faithfully implementing the required reading curriculum, but you receive different corrective feedback from building administrators, district administrators, curriculum experts, and professional developers. Your mentors and colleagues down the hall offer a different set of advice. It would not be surprising if, eventually, you conclude that you will have to resolve the conflicting information and create methods of reading instruction that, to the best of your ability, represent a sound approach to reading. Add to this challenge the reality that veteran reading teachers may be more experienced and expert than many new administrators in the nuances of reading instruction, and you have a formula for poor morale and, most important, inconsistent opportunities for students.

It is essential to note that there is no malice here. In observations of thousands of teachers, I have yet to meet one whose heart's desire was poor instruction. Even when teachers are engaging in practices that are discredited by research and contrary to clear instructions from the district leadership, the reasons are sometimes found not in willful insubordination but in conflicting instructions from multiple authorities and conflicting demands from advocates of different academic disciplines. Each time literacy instruction is interrupted by administrative announcements or the "nonnegotiable" time allocated to literacy is reduced to make way for the priority of the day, teachers recognize that the gulf between leaders' words and actions is wide indeed.

The Leadership Challenge

Effective instruction is a profoundly important variable for improving student achievement and educational equity (Marzano, Pickering, &

Pollock, 2001; Reeves, 2006b), and administrators have been exhorted to monitor instruction more closely with walk-throughs (Cervone & Martinez-Miller, 2007; Downey, Steffy, English, Frase, & Poston, 2004) and other supervisory techniques. But administrators can walk marathons through the hallways and classrooms of a school and accomplish nothing if they do not begin with a clear and consistent idea of what effective instruction looks like and have the ability to communicate the elements of effective instruction in clear and unmistakable terms. Most of all, instructional leaders must consider not only the apparent compliance with instructional protocols but also the evidence that students are learning.

Therefore, leaders have three essential challenges related to improving literacy instruction and, as a result, improving student learning in every subject. First, leaders must make the case for consistency in reading instruction. Interestingly, the same teachers and leaders whose definitions of effective reading instruction varied widely were nearly unanimous (more than 98 percent of respondents) in concluding that consistency in reading instruction was "extremely important." This is particularly true when the conversation turns to the expectations of instruction from teachers responsible for the immediately preceding year. For example, 2nd grade teachers may disagree about what their curriculum should be, but they have no difficulty expecting 1st grade teachers to deliver a consistent literacy curriculum. Consistent literacy instruction is not a reflection of central office mandates or federal funding requirements, but a reflection of the value of equal opportunity for literacy success for all students.

Second, leaders must define in clear and specific terms what "good teaching" really means. The best way to do this is the creation of a scoring guide—from novice to progressing to proficient to expert—for each element of instruction (Marshall, 2006). This scoring guide is more than a checklist that reflects that guided reading was taking place at the appropriate time of day. Rather, leaders must know and communicate the difference between an expert and a novice approach to guided reading and every other element of reading instruction. These norms should be so clear and specific that teachers can monitor their own practice and observe their colleagues and almost always come to the same conclusion about the level of instruction as an administrator. This focus on effective literacy instruction is not the exclusive province of the time officially designated for reading in elementary school or for language arts teachers in secondary school. As Ness (2007) reminds us, instruction in math, science, and social studies will benefit significantly when students have access to literacy instruction in multiple contexts.

Third, leaders must balance the need for consistency on essentials with the necessary differentiation to meet student needs. A scoring guide of professional practices is more complex than a checklist and takes more than a few minutes to complete. But the extra effort devoted now to define the elements of literacy instruction across a continuum of performance is the best way to provide the clarity that teachers need and students deserve. The progress of the past decade in research on literacy has little effect if leaders resort to simply repeating slogans and purchasing programs. If educational leaders believe that literacy is the priority that they claim it to be, then they have a personal responsibility to understand literacy instruction, to define it for their colleagues, and to observe it on a daily basis.

Finally, leaders and teachers must collaborate to find the golden mean between instruction that is compliant but devoid of joy and classroom practices that are fun but unsupported by research. Allington (2005) reminds us that although consistency on the essentials of literacy instruction is important, expert teaching of reading is not following a script but rather is based on a bone-deep commitment to proficiency for every student: "Good teaching, effective teaching, is not just about using whatever science says 'usually' works best. It is all about finding out what works best for the individual child and the group of children in front of you" (p. 462).

PART 4

Sustaining Change

Implementing change requires focus, clarity, and monitoring—qualities that will place you among the very best change leaders in the world. Unfortunately, even superior accomplishments in focus, clarity, and monitoring are insufficient to sustain change. Indeed, most change efforts emphasize individual and organizational effectiveness—necessary but not sufficient conditions for sustainable change.

To sustain change, leaders must refocus their energies beyond the attainment of short-term effectiveness and look toward the greater good (Hargreaves & Fink, 2006; Reeves & Allison, 2009; Wheatley & Frieze, 2007). Here is the acid test question for sustainability: if funding evaporated and administrative mandates were withdrawn, would this change endure? That is precisely what happened in Norfolk, Virginia, with the use of Focus Schools (Reeves, 2008), when schools voluntarily participated in a remarkably effective change leadership program long after administrative requirements had been withdrawn.

The challenge of persistent change without administrative mandates may seem daunting enough, but consider this: if you knew that you had to make a massive change, but you would have to do so with the same staff, the same contract, the same rewards, and the same institutional structure that you have now, could you do it? That is precisely what happened in a school district in California, as described in Chapter 14. Despite overwhelming poverty and a long history of low performance, changes in leadership and the replacement of a small minority of staff members led to major improvements in student results.

Lessons in sustainable change have global applications and come from global sources, as described in Chapter 15. Far from highways and electricity, the Shamombo School in rural Zambia offers lessons in which leadership, culture, and commitment combine to survive crushing poverty, political upheaval, and devastating diseases.

In Chapter 16, we travel halfway around the world from Zambia to Jenks, Oklahoma, where we are reminded that administrative leadership is necessary but not sufficient for sustainable change; leadership in the most effective schools comes also from teachers. Teacher leadership, however, is often stymied by tradition, culture, and a history in which "teacher leadership" was little more than a euphemism for the assignment of administrative duties to teachers without accompanying compensation. In other cases, teacher leaders filled a vacuum left by ineffective administrators. Jenks defies these stereotypes, showing that strong and effective administrative leaders not only coexist with but also depend upon effective teacher leaders. Together, administrators and teachers in Jenks tackled one of the most intractable changes in contemporary education—the schedule and course assignments in comprehensive high schools. In yet another example of short-term change with stunningly effective results, this team of leaders overcame the skeptics to deliver hope and opportunity for students.

We close this section and the book with a new view of educational accountability. As this book goes to press, the United States and several other countries are entering a new era of educational accountability. Although test-driven accountability can be dated to the Ming Dynasty (1368–1644) and, some might argue, to the first multiple-choice test in the Garden of Eden, the lessons of history do not seem to be learned as frequently as they are taught. The few moments spent on a single test need not define our lives, and a new approach to accountability can have as its central messages insight and resilience rather than judgment and labeling. Whether or not national policymakers apply these lessons, whether or not your system maintains a narrowly focused view of accountability, every educator and school leader can create a broader vision of accountability for their classroom and school. Sustainable change, after all, depends not upon compliance with external mandates or blind adherence to regulation, but rather upon the pursuit of the greater good.

Consider two questions. When you were in 2nd grade, what were the national, state, provincial, and local accountability systems for your school? Doesn't ring a bell, does it? Try this one: when you were in 2nd grade, what made you most proud and happy in the classroom? Chances are, you recall a room rich in color, full of laughter, alive with the joy of learning. You mastered some skills that seemed challenging just the year before, and you gained confidence as a learner. Most of all, you knew *every* day—not just on test day—that you were learning. Those memories are an important foundation as we consider educational accountability in the years ahead. Although political variables may be beyond our control, at least in the immediate term, the decisions we make every day will determine what accountability really means in the eyes of our students and communities.

14

Sustaining Excellence

It's not hard to find examples of short-term success in high-poverty schools. Such cases have been documented in the recent work of Chenoweth (2007) and in my own studies of 90/90/90 schools—those with 90 percent poverty, 90 percent minority enrollment, and 90 percent of students meeting or exceeding academic standards (Reeves, 2004b). Earlier studies by Edmonds (1979), Haycock (1999), and Carter (1999) also identified schools that were succeeding despite the fact that they enrolled large numbers of students in poverty.

These case studies are admirable and amazing. But when I share them with classroom teachers and education leaders, they typically respond, "Great! Those ideas worked in one place at one time. Why should I believe that they'll work in my school, or that such success will last?" Critics of these studies have questioned whether schools can consistently overcome the pervasive effects of poverty, language, and other conditions that influence student learning (Rothstein, 2004). In the face of continuing challenges, can high-poverty schools really achieve long-term academic excellence? The case of Mead Valley Elementary School suggests that sustained excellence is possible even in the face of profound demographic challenges.

Mead Valley's Challenges

Located in the Val Verde Unified School District in Riverside County, California, Mead Valley is among the poorest schools in the United States. More than 95 percent of the students are eligible for free or reduced-price lunch, and more than 70 percent are English language learners. The area has high rates of drug abuse and violent crime. Evidence of poverty is stark and pervasive: some homes and trailers lack sewage services; dead animals lie in the streets unattended; many children are chronically hungry. Yet in this environment, the school has sustained a level of educational excellence that transcends student demographics, transitions in teaching staff, and changes in school leadership.

A Culture of Commitment

Some schools that have been labeled as "successful" engage in a particularly disturbing practice. They focus on improving the performance of students who, with a bit of intensive intervention, can get to proficiency. The unfortunate result of this strategy—called "triage" in some circles—is that students performing significantly below grade level are treated as being beyond hope, and those performing far above the proficiency cutoff are neglected.

Mead Valley's strategy is quite different. The school has a clear commitment to all students, including the "far below basic" students whom some schools ignore. This culture of commitment extends to all members of the school community, including not only administrators and teachers, but also the noncertified staff. This is a school in which custodians, bus drivers, and cafeteria workers all take pride in student success, questioning, challenging, and encouraging students at every opportunity. According to former principal Earl Shore, the key is "more minutes of teacher-student interaction for every student." As Shore describes it, the success of Mead Valley appears to be the result of a combination of practices and people.

Practices and People

The professional practices successfully applied at Mead Valley are clearly defined and potentially replicable. But to be effective over time, they require a notable degree of schoolwide dedication and consistency.

The first strategy was to develop common curricula and assessments for all students at all grades levels, greatly reducing the variation in teacher expectations from one classroom to the next. The school uses a combination of home-grown and externally developed common assessments. The key, Shore suggests, is using assessments that are consistently more rigorous than the final, state assessment.

Second, the school sets aside three hours of "sacred time" each day for literacy. There are no pullouts or peripheral activities to interrupt students' most important task—learning to read and write in English. The school uses the prescribed reading texts and also incorporates specific interventions for English language learners. In addition, students practice writing daily and write for publication—that is, a perfect final draft after multiple revisions on a single topic—at least once a month. Faculty meetings reflect a similar focus, with a discussion of all available data on students, including not only test scores but also recent teacher observations, identification of students in need of intervention, and discussion of the faculty's most effective teaching practices. Initially, some teachers resisted this idea and clung to what Schmoker (2001) calls "the Crayola curriculum." Shore explains, "We love the arts, and you can see them all around the school, but we don't do arts and crafts during sacred literacy time."

Third, the school builds emotional confidence for students and faculty. Regular ceremonies of recognition and reward throughout the year send the message that this is a place where students can thrive, irrespective of conditions outside the school. Seven years ago the school had a culture of defeat and a sense of hopelessness, according to Shore. Today, teachers have relentless enthusiasm and confidence. This confidence is reflected in daily discussions focused on student success. Thus the principle of "sacred time" applies not only to literacy but also to teacher discussions that focus exclusively on improving student achievement.

Fourth, the school sets and enforces standards of professional responsibility. Inadequate teaching is not tolerated. The people who pay the biggest price for poor teaching are students and other teachers, who must do extra work if another teacher is not up to the task. Of the 27 teachers at Mead Valley, 3 were terminated and 2 transferred at the end of the first year of Mr. Shore's change initiatives. This level of teacher turnover is not unusual in exceptionally challenging schools. This step can be an emotional, legal, and financial challenge for a school system. But effective instructional leadership depends on recognizing and rewarding professional excellence and, when necessary, eliminating ineffective practice. Decisions about contract renewal, transfers, performance improvement, and terminations can be particularly difficult when staff members have grown accustomed to poor learning and teaching conditions. Nevertheless, effective schools have absolute clarity about the characteristics of effective literacy instruction, faculty collaboration, student assessment, and meaningful intervention. Failure to meet these professional standards need not be a subjective judgment but a judgment that results from a clear comparison of actual to expected performance. In fact, although it is tempting to focus on the few teachers who were dismissed, it is more remarkable to note that to a very large degree, the same teachers were in the school during this period of sustained excellence. It was different practices, leadership, and commitment—not just different people— that made the difference.

The concept of "sacred time" also applies to teacher collaboration. Every Wednesday, the students leave at 12:30 p.m., and teachers meet from 1:00 to 3:00 p.m. to focus on student achievement, content, and teaching strategies. The meetings follow clear and specific norms, including universal participation and a focus on the learning agenda. The agenda is clear and consistent. The school has established clear achievement targets for every student, for every class, and for the entire school. For example, at the end of the year, every kindergartner should be able to write three sentences; every 3rd grader, three paragraphs; and every 5th grader, five paragraphs.

Sustained Results

In California, the Academic Performance Index (API) measures student performance in English language arts and mathematics. In 2000, Mead Valley's API was 450. By 2004, it had jumped to 695. In many cases, such a dramatic improvement is followed by flat or declining scores, but Mead Valley's record of sustained excellence is reflected in the scores for subsequent years: 729 in 2005, 746 in 2006, and 774 in 2007. Special education students and English language learners also made substantial gains. In fall 2007, the school was named a California Distinguished School for the first time in its history. The school is poised to break 800, an API score more commonly associated with wealthy suburban schools. What is particularly noteworthy about these scores is that the last gain happened after Shore left to take a position as assistant superintendent. The new principal, Ruth Salazar, fully embraced the culture of commitment and successful professional practices, proving that even after the leader departs, culture and instructional strategies can endure.

Replicating Success

Can Mead Valley's success be replicated? I believe the answer is an emphatic *yes*, for three compelling reasons. First, the techniques used in this school were not idiosyncratic, but rather were culled from the research on the 90/90/90 schools and other sources. Mead Valley did not invent these strategies but learned from the practices of other successful high-poverty schools. Second, the strategies were not the result of a short burst of energy by a few people who soon burned out, but were sustained over more than half a decade. Third and most important, although some staff turnover occurred—something that happens frequently in high-poverty schools that are not making any changes—a significant number of staff members remained at the school and were part of its successful turnaround. These are the same kind of good people and hardworking professionals who are in many challenging schools, but with new practices and a culture of commitment, the same people produced dramatically improved results.

15

Lessons Across the Globe

Recently I traveled to rural Zambia to dedicate a school that my colleagues and I had built there. Combining the proceeds of the Brock International Prize with private donations, we were able to fund the Shamombo School through the Makangua Area Development Program. Although the funding and initial support came from private donors and nongovernmental organizations (in this case, World Vision), the ownership and control of the school is entirely within the purview of the Zambian Ministry of Education and the local governing board of parents, teachers, and community leaders. Amid the celebration of a facility that will serve more than 550 students in grades 1 through 9, I learned some leadership lessons.

The situation in Zambia is complex. Many schools are dilapidated —the new school replaced one that was more than 40 years old, was falling apart, and had been condemned by the Zambian government. Parent support is inconsistent. Too many children stay away from school either because they are caring for an ailing parent or because they must work in the fields for relatives who see little value in education, particularly for girls. An estimated 20 percent of the students have HIV/AIDS, and up to one-third either have been orphaned by the disease or have parents suffering from it.

Although the curriculum is prescribed, its application is inconsistent. Teachers are scarce and misallocated. In 2006–2007, Shamombo School had 5 teachers serving 476 students; in 2007–2008, 12 teachers will serve more than 550 students. The doubling of the teaching staff allows the school to work in double shifts rather than triple shifts, but with the increasing student population, triple shifts will probably return in the future. Teacher training ranges from the exemplary to the wholly inadequate; the teachers college I visited was trying desperately to keep up with the demand despite a lack of books, supplies, and teacher mentors. The pay for teachers and principals is dismal, and many educators leave the profession early in their career.

Despite the challenges of poor facilities, large class sizes, inadequate parent support, inconsistent curriculum, and widely varying teacher training (sound familiar?), the education and community leaders of the Makangua region, in which Shamombo is located, taught me several valuable lessons.

"Anything to Add or Subtract?"

Meetings were conducted with uncommon civility. In this region, where chiefs and headmen remain dominant political forces alongside (and sometimes superior to) government officials, local community governance is an emerging art. Observations of meetings regarding school curriculum, community health, plans for improved water supplies, and teacher preparation showed remarkable consistencies in the conduct of affairs. People speak thoughtfully, courteously, and seriously, with clear focus on the issue at hand. Women, whose voices only recently have been heard in community and government councils in the region, are encouraged to contribute and speak, even when they have not asked for recognition. At the end of every meeting, the leader asks, "Is there anything to add or subtract from our meeting?" How often I have wished that I could have not only added to the content of a meeting but also subtracted a comment I made in haste, a cutting remark, an unkind word, or a premature judgment.

"What Do You Need to Learn?"

When my friend Victor Simuchimba started school at age 12, he was not asked, "What grade are you in?" or "How old are you?" Rather, he was asked, "What do you need to learn?" Because his father had died and the uncle with whom he lived required him to work for his family's housing and food, Victor did not attend school until he could leave his uncle's home. When he explained that he had never held a book or a pencil and did not know anything but his native language, he was placed in the 1st grade. Victor stayed in school for 12 years, finishing high school at the age of 24. How logical is it that state funding formulas and hidebound tradition conspire to associate the age of a student with a grade level, rather than recognizing that the relevant question for every student is "What do you need to learn?" Before you tell me that such a question would lead to overwhelming complexity and your school system could not possibly deal with it, please be prepared to explain why your system is more complex and challenging than that of Zambia.

"We Are So Grateful"

One of the most wonderful things about Africa is the music. In every corner of the most remote and impoverished areas I visited, the sounds of four-part harmony would greet my arrival and punctuate every meeting. The singing was lyrical and accompanied by joyful dancing. I was particularly moved at a meeting of one particular HIV/AIDS support group, at which members gathered to help one another manage their medications and learn about preventing the spread of the disease that is the scourge of Africa. Even in such a bleak setting, I easily became lost in the harmonies and rhythms of the singers—at least until my hostess, Madame Nkomo, asked if I knew what they were singing. I shook my head, so she translated the lyrics of the refrain: "We are so grateful. We are so grateful. We are so grateful." It made no sense to my Western ears. I was angry at social injustice, furious with the slow pace of medical treatment, frustrated and bewildered that the developing world could find millions of dollars to extract Zambian copper and just pennies to pay Zambian teachers. Thus, I could not understand this song, literally or emotionally.

But if I am to learn the lessons of Shamombo, then I must do more than be angry when confronted with the challenges in Africa—or in the schools that I work in today. The obstacles that teachers and education leaders confront are immense, but we can choose our refrain. Will it be one of anger, complaint, cynicism, and despair? The lessons of Shamombo suggest that we can choose instead to learn from African students, teachers, and leaders who face hardship every day, and let our refrain be "We are so grateful."

16

Teacher Leadership

Teacher leadership is a concept that extends far beyond a slogan and has become an integral part of education reform. It is no coincidence that award-winning school districts have made teacher leadership a key part of their strategies for continued success. Another characteristic of such school districts is their insistence on continuous improvement. Consider the case of Jenks Public Schools in Oklahoma, winner of the 2005 Baldrige Award for school quality. The cooperative efforts of teachers and administrators have led to remarkable progress for some of the most challenging students in the system.

Intervening to Prevent Failure

Although Jenks has enjoyed a history of academic success, the district recognized that too many students continued to face failure. The faculty of Jenks High School worked together to find the most accurate early-warning indicators that students might fail courses. For example, when they considered the factors that predicted failure in math, the faculty learned that any 9th grade student who earned a *D* in English or math and also failed a criterion-referenced reading or math test was almost certain to fail his or her next math course. That's right—trouble in reading is a clear predictor not only of trouble in future English courses but also of trouble in future math courses. In the past, these students would not have received intervention until after failing one or more 9th grade courses. Now Jenks uses its data analysis to intervene to prevent failure.

The strategies that Jenks uses have three striking characteristics. First, intervention is proactive, not reactive. Even if a student is earning a D and therefore not yet failing, Jenks intervenes; it does not wait for a failing grade to institute intervention strategies. Second, intervention is delivered by outstanding faculty members. In a remarkable example of teacher leadership, expert faculty members, including those who have taught advanced placement courses to the school's most successful students, have volunteered to take on the classes of the school's most challenging students. Third, intervention strategies include time—twice the number of classroom contact hours than had been provided in the past. These interventions are mandatory for students who need them. Teachers and administrators are relentless in their determination that all students will succeed—even students who resist the requirements imposed on them to prevent failure.

Of course, extra time alone does not ensure success, but time is a crucial variable. Even great teachers equipped with excellent curriculum cannot erase a multiyear deficit in learning unless students have the time necessary to acquire essential background knowledge and also master grade-level requirements. For example, students who need intervention in English receive not only the regular grade-level course but also an extra class in reading and composition. In math, students receive not only the regular Algebra I class but also an Algebra Lab class in which they are taught the essentials of number operations, problem solving, and analysis.

The results speak for themselves. In the regular math classes populated by students who had no apparent need for intervention, 38 percent of the students received a grade of A or B and 36 percent received a C. In the Math Lab classes, populated by students who started the semester significantly behind their peers and were considered at high risk of failure, 46 percent earned an A or a B and 25 percent earned a C. Lest skeptical readers attribute this performance to positive bias on the part of the lab teachers, consider the following: on the state math exam, 42 percent of the students enrolled in the lab classes scored at the Advanced or Satisfactory levels, compared with 20 percent of students enrolled in regular classes.

What is the secret of this award-winning system? Superintendent Kirby Lehman said in an interview that he credits teacher leadership. "Outstanding teachers have chosen to be directly involved in the remedial courses," he noted. "We are making the correct decision by doubling the time for our high-challenge students in both math and language arts and using the best instructors available to provide such remediation."

By intervening decisively and immediately—before failure takes place—Jenks High School has already achieved a dramatic reduction in failures. The superintendent's comment on this success is particularly telling: "We are not yet satisfied with the results." Dr. Lehman and his colleagues will not be content until students achieve 100 percent proficiency.

Does Intervention Hurt Electives?

Whenever a school provides extra time for students and teachers to prevent failure, the short-term effect on elective courses is inevitably a source of controversy. Students who take an algebra lab, a composition class, or a reading course are losing a 9th grade elective. Of course, students who fail English and algebra courses and then retake those classes as 10th and 11th grade students are losing electives in these grades, often with increasing levels of frustration for teacher and student alike. As the results from Jenks make clear, preventing failures in 9th grade leads to fewer course repetitions later in high school.

Leadership at Every Level

In their determination to help struggling students succeed, Jenks and many other schools face challenges that cannot be addressed by one more program, inspirational speaker, or administrative command. Their success is the result of great leadership, to be sure. But leadership in these systems takes place at every level, including leadership by example from teachers who place the interests of students first.

Epilogue: The Risks and Rewards of Change

Like an attorney at the end of a contentious trial, I now have an opportunity for a closing argument. My clients, the educators and school leaders you have met in the preceding pages, have offered strong evidence about effective change leadership. The decision before you, as with every member of a jury, depends on whether you consider the evidence credible, compelling, and a sufficient rationale for your final decision. The problem, of course, is that juries can make mistakes. They rarely have perfect information, and they almost always listen to thoughtful advocates—the lawyers on the other side of a question— who also offer persuasive testimony that the jury should come to a different conclusion. How will you decide the case before you?

The Standard of Evidence

First, juries have standards of evidence. Perhaps one side has power-ful testimony of individual experiences. These stories, often full of personal detail and strong emotion, can be very compelling. In the context of change, these stories sometimes begin, "We tried that at my school, and it didn't work." Sometimes the personal experience is not directly related, but it remains heartfelt and persuasively presented, such as those who contend, "This new idea is just a different name for what we tried 20 years ago, and that old idea has been completely discredited." Perhaps the most frequent argument against change is based on the personal beliefs and unique contexts of the witnesses: "I don't care what the articles and studies say about other places; if you didn't study my school and my students, how do I know it will work here?"

Fortunately, judges instruct juries to use a standard when considering alternative sources of evidence. In a criminal case, the standard is that the evidence to convict a defendant must be "beyond a reasonable doubt." In a civil case, two standards are employed. The first is that the prevailing party must show "the preponderance of the evidence." Carlson, Imwinkelried, and Kionka (1991) note, "There must be a preponderance of evidence in favor of the party who has the burden of proof. . . . [T]he greater weight or preponderance of evidence does not necessarily mean the greater quantity of evidence or the larger number of witnesses but is the greater weight of proof" (p. 995).

The second standard is that of "clear and convincing proof" (p. 996), a phrase that is used synonymously with the phrases "clear, precise and indubitable," "clear conviction without hesitation," and "clear, satisfactory, and convincing" (p. 996). This significantly higher standard of proof is used in cases that include criminal and civil actions, in examples such as eyewitness testimony and evidence obtained during warrantless searches. Notice that the evidentiary standard for the jury is never one of "scientific certainty." Therefore, as the juror in this case, you are not required to assess the evidence in the previous chapters and ask, "Is this a scientific certainty? Will it work every time as an immutable law of the physical universe?" By such a standard, every juror would be paralyzed, cases would never be resolved, and change in school or any other organization would never happen. Rather, you are simply asked to choose which of two sides of every argument has the better evidence. And what you decide is "better" will not be based on the quantity of people arguing the case or their emotional intensity, but rather the depth, breadth, and consistency of the evidence.

In this book and the reference section that supports it, you clearly have the preponderance of evidence on your side. In many cases, I would argue that the evidence is clear and convincing. For example, you have

• Evidence from different research perspectives, including a variety of quantitative and qualitative methods.

• Evidence from different student demographic groups, including groups with high and low levels of poverty, high and low minority enrollment, and high and low second-language enrollment.

• Evidence from different geographical areas, including schools throughout the United States and Canada, as well as an example from Africa. My colleagues and I are already gathering data from schools in South America, Asia, Europe, and Australia to ensure that future editions are even more comprehensive.

• Evidence from different researchers. Although much of the work presented in this book stems from my work directly in schools around the world, the conclusions are always bolstered with evidence from other scholars. The evidence before you, therefore, is not the collected war stories of one educator, but rather a variety of evidence from a variety of sources and methods. When you compare it to evidence that opposes the change initiatives offered in these pages, there is little doubt which side has met the evidentiary burden.

Whether you are considering how to improve literacy achievement, increase attendance, reform your grading system, inspire your staff, reconstitute your accountability policy, or engage in any number of reforms addressed in this book, you need not ponder the question endlessly. Any reasonable jury should be able to evaluate the evidence and then consider the best course of action. Unfortunately, juries do not always reach such clear-cut decisions based on the evidence.

What If the Jury Is Deadlocked?

When a unanimous decision is required, such as in a criminal trial, even a single juror can prevent the other 11 jurors from reaching a conclusion. In some jurisdictions, for a civil case only 9 of 12 jurors must come to a conclusion to resolve the case, thus allowing 4 out of 12—only 33 percent—to stop the decision-making process in its tracks. Sometimes the jury is deadlocked because of a single person who is wracked by conscience and full of doubt, and we revere the character made famous by Henry Fonda in *Twelve Angry Men* for maintaining his position in the face of opposition. Other cases involve a single recalcitrant juror who ignores the evidence, injects personal bias, fears community reaction to an unpopular verdict, or disregards the conclusions of the majority of the jury for reasons having nothing to do with the evidence at hand. Sometimes the jurors are fearful of making a mistake, as either decision in a case will lead to an adverse consequence for someone.

When a jury is deadlocked, only two choices are available. The first is the so-called hung jury, a deliberative body that is unable to consider the evidence before it and come to a conclusion. The second and most common choice is for the judge to instruct the jurors to continue to deliberate, try again, examine the evidence, use their own skills and abilities, work harder, and then come to a conclusion. In the vast majority of cases, their hard work pays off. The jurors work longer, reason through the evidence, consider multiple points of view, and ultimately follow their duty to make a decision based on the best evidence they have available. What the jury never is permitted to do is to simply wait endlessly in the jury room until perfect evidence arrives. They must render a decision based on the evidence at hand.

In many education debates, we must now decide whether we as teachers, leaders, policymakers, and citizens shall be a hung jury, waiting for evidentiary perfection as another generation of students fails to receive the improved opportunities that the changes in these pages might provide to them. Note the word *might* in the previous sentence, because although the evidence in this book is strong, it is not—it cannot be—scientific certainty. When someone says, "Can you guarantee me that nonfiction writing will improve science achievement?" or "Can you promise that the new grading system will reduce failures?" the answers are invariably in the negative. The same, of course, is true if the parent asks, "Can you promise me that this polio vaccination will protect my child from polio?" Again, the sad answer is no—but I can promise that both your child and children throughout the community are safer if your child receives the vaccination, even as I acknowledge that approximately one out of every 2.4 million students who receives that vaccine will have an adverse reaction to it—perhaps even suffering from polio. If we allowed that probability to halt the distribution of polio vaccine, however, then we would return to the 1940s and 1950s, when stunning numbers of children were afflicted by a disease that left them with atrophied limbs and damaged lungs. The absence of certainty does not stop good public policy in either medicine or education.

Your Choice of Mistakes

At the conclusion of your deliberations, members of the jury, you do not have a choice of perfection. Rather, you must choose one of two mistakes. The first mistake is that you will enact vital educational changes even though they will sometimes be ineffective and unnecessary. Having made this mistake, you will suffer the criticism of cynics who, a year later, say, "See, I told you we didn't need that!"

The second mistake is that you will fail to enact vital educational changes, and another year, two years—perhaps a generation—will pass before someone else will use the same information that you had and will, at last, enact the changes that you considered. Leaders at every level, along with a generation of students, will at that time ask, "Why didn't you do this earlier?"

The final question therefore is not "How do we make perfect decisions?" Rather, the essential question is "How do we choose the wiser mistake to make?" The first mistake—enacting change that is not perfectly effective—will leave you vulnerable to criticism and complaint from the same chorus of cynics who avoid progress now just as surely as they delayed the end of corporal punishment a generation ago. The evidence was clear, but the educational juries of the day remained deadlocked, unable to come to a conclusion. Juries who surrendered to those critics chose community and peer popularity over their duty, and children paid the price. Failing to act when the evidence suggests you must may safeguard you from the catcalls of cynics, but such a mistake will expose you to judgment, years hence, from the students and communities you failed to help.

I have done my best to assemble the evidence and submit it for your consideration as the jurors of today. Your choice is not perfection, but a choice of two mistakes: action or inaction, evidence or speculation, criticism from cynics or criticism from a future generation. Choose wisely.

Appendix A: Support Documents for Creating Conditions for Systemic Change

This appendix consists of the following documents:
- Change Initiative History
- Change Literature Synthesis and Discussion
- Why School Change Fails
- Assumptions Basic to Successful Educational Change
- Questions to Ask Yourself as You Contemplate a Change Initiative
- Focus Group Questions on Change Readiness
- Change Readiness Continuum
- Change Readiness Continuum Rubric
- Stakeholder Change Readiness Matrix

The author is deeply indebted to Dr. Mike Wasta, former superintendent of the Bristol Public Schools in Connecticut and now a change leadership consultant. His insights and expertise contributed immeasurably to this work. These documents may be reproduced by school systems for noncommercial use. Free downloads of these documents are also available at www.ChangeLeaders.info.

Change Initiative History

Instructions: Use this form to guide a discussion of the change history in your school or system. Use a separate copy of this form for each change that you review. For each change, identify what went right and what went wrong. A synthesis of this discussion should lead to a list of your own "lessons learned" for effective change.

Previous change initiative:

_____

_____

_____

What Went Right	What Went Wrong

Change Literature Synthesis and Discussion

The three works used in this activity are John Kotter's (2006) *Leading Change*, Michael Fullan's (2008) *The Six Secrets of Change*, and Charles Reigeluth's (2006) *The Guidance System for Transforming Education*.

In *Leading Change*, Kotter describes what he believes are the eight stages that any successful change initiative must evolve through if it is to be successful and sustained. The eight stages that he describes are fairly straightforward and need no explanation.

In *The Six Secrets of Change*, Fullan describes the six conditions that he believes must be present in any organization for change to be successful and sustained. His six secrets require some explanation:

- **Love Your Employees.** Invest in the development and well-being of your employees.
- **Connect Peers with Purpose.** Foster continuous and purposeful peer interaction.
- **Capacity Building Prevails.** Invest in the development of individual and collaborative efficacy of a whole group or system to accomplish significant improvements.
- **Learning Is the Work.** View *working* and *learning to work better* as one and the same.
- **Transparency Rules.** Clearly and continuously share results and the practices that led to the results.
- **Systems Learn.** The system learns from itself on a continuous basis. People in the system learn new things all the time.

Charles Reigeluth is less well-known than Kotter and Fullan, but he has done extensive work in the area of moving a school district through a profound change process. Reigeluth's *Guidance System for*

Transforming Education includes six steps presented in a sequential fashion. Like Kotter's, the steps are self-explanatory.

The point of this exercise is to have the reader gain a general idea of the thinking of significant researchers in the field and to recognize the convergence of their thinking. Although not perfectly aligned, the similarities between Kotter's guiding coalition and Reigeluth's starter team are striking, as is the strong need for capacity building expressed in each theory. Finally, each theory cites the need to "anchor the new approach in the culture" or make sure the "systems learn" or "implement and evolve the system."

If this exercise is going to stand alone, more detail, such as that cited above, will be needed. Reading all three authors would be ideal but perhaps unrealistic.

Kotter	Fullan	Reigeluth
Sense of urgency	Love employees	Systemic change
Guiding coalition	Connect peers with purpose	Starter team
Vision and strategy	Capacity building prevails	Capacity for change
Communicate the vision	Learning is the work	Designs for new schools
Empowering action	Transparency rules	Implement and evolve
Short-term wins	Systems learn	
Consolidating gains		
Anchor new approach in existing culture		

Discussion: What do these research findings have in common?

_____

_____

_____

_____

_____

_____

Why School Change Fails

Kurt Squire and Charles Reigeluth

[T]he most important outcome of any fundamental change process must be a change in the stakeholders' mindsets and beliefs about education. Without changes in the users' mindsets, no fundamental change is likely to succeed. (Squire & Reigeluth, 2000, p. 150)

John Goodlad

One of the major reasons why schools don't change much is that change needs leadership. It needs committed, intelligent leadership, an agenda, an awareness of the conditions that have to be in place and a grasp of the strategies that one has to use to effect change. (Goldberg, 2000, p. 84)

Change requires leadership over a long period of time, and most school leaders don't stay in the job long enough to effect change. (Goldberg, 2000, pp. 84–85)

If you are going to engage in a significant process of renewal, there must be a continuing critical mass of people who are committed to the agenda, who are willing to spend the time and who get rewarded for spending the time. (Goldberg, 2000, p. 85)

Peter Senge and Associates

The fundamental flaw in most innovators' strategies is that they focus on their innovations, on what they are trying to do—rather than on understanding how the larger culture, structures and norms will react to their efforts. (Senge et al., 1999, p. 26)

Michael Fullan

Educational change fails partly because of the assumptions of planners and partly because solving substantial problems is an inherently complex business. The characteristics of the change, the makeup of the local district, the character of individual schools and teachers, and the existence and form of external relationships interact to produce conditions for change or no change. It takes a fortunate combination of the right factors—a critical mass—to support and guide the process of relearning, which respects the maintenance needs of individuals and groups and at the same time facilitates, stimulates, and prods people to change through a process of incremental and decremental fits and starts on the way to institutionalizing (or, if appropriate, rejecting) the change in question. Single-factor theories of change are doomed to failure. (Fullan, 2007, p. 26)

Looking at the preceding quotes, synthesize the comments into one sentence about *why school change fails*:

———————————————————————

———————————————————————

———————————————————————

———————————————————————

———————————————————————

———————————————————————

———————————————————————

———————————————————————

Assumptions Basic to Successful Educational Change

1. Do not assume that your version of what the change should be is the one that should or could be implemented.

2. Assume that any significant innovation, if it is to result in change, requires individual implementers to work out their own meaning.

3. Assume that conflict and disagreement are not only inevitable but fundamental to successful change.

4. Assume that people need pressure to change, but it will be effective only under conditions that allow them to react, form their own positions, interact with other implementers, obtain assistance, and develop new capacities.

5. Assume that effective change takes time.

6. Do not assume that the reason for lack of implementation is outright rejection of the value embodied in the change, or hard-core resistance.

7. Do not expect all or even most groups to change.

8. Assume that you will need a plan that is based on the above assumptions and that addresses the factors known to affect implementation.

9. Assume that no amount of knowledge will ever make totally clear what action should be taken.

10. Assume that changing the culture of institutions is the real agenda, not implementing single innovations. (Fullan, 2007)

Questions to Ask Yourself as You Contemplate a Change Initiative

1. What skills will the people charged with implementing the change need? Do they have these skills? If not, how will they acquire them?

2. How much training will be needed? Where will we get the training? How much will it cost? Where will we get the funding?

3. How are parents likely to feel about the change?

4. If we start to receive some push-back, what is the board of education likely to do?

5. How will we approach the teachers union so that they don't just react negatively?

6. How can we develop the political support we will need to see this change through?

7. Am I, as the change catalyst, prepared to stay here for the several years it is likely to take to embed this change in the culture?

8. How are we going to develop a plan that will allow us to deal with the issues we can't possibly anticipate beforehand?

9. Are there skills that I, as the change catalyst, need to acquire before I attempt this change?

What other questions might you add?

_____

_____

_____

_____

_____

_____

_____

_____

Focus Group Questions on Change Readiness

Focus groups provide a qualitative context for researchers. Through rich discussions and detailed narratives, we can learn the "story behind the numbers." Ideally, focus groups extend a wide reach to many different stakeholders, including not only teachers, administrators, parents, and students, but also other groups that may not respond to typical surveys and calls. At the Leadership and Learning Center, for example, we make a point to conduct focus groups with parents in the language they are most likely to speak at home. We also provide child care, transportation, and food—essentials if the purpose of the focus group research is to hear from a wide variety of constituents.

One important consideration in focus group research is confidentiality. Therefore, it is almost always essential that an independent researcher is engaged who can provide absolute independence from the school system and confidentiality to the group participants. When local administrators say, "It's OK—be honest with me—say whatever is on your mind," it is a nice gesture. Nevertheless, it is almost certain that sometime within living memory of most focus group participants, that candor was rewarded with a dictatorial manager who shot the messenger. Therefore, the use of an independent facilitator for focus groups is not an indication of distrust of the present leadership of the school system but is a carryover of decades of distrust that preceded the current administration.

The following questions are designed to begin a discussion that will address the stakeholder group's attitude toward the domain. The facilitator should use the questions to draw out the group members while someone else records the responses. After the session, the facilitator and the recorder should immediately review their notes and use the Rubric (p. 160) to rate each stakeholder group's responses on the Continuum (p. 159).

History

1. What past or current change efforts can you recall?
2. What did you think about each?
3. How comfortable are you with change in general?

Need for Change

4. Is there a need for improvement in your schools?
5. What are you most dissatisfied with?
6. What changes would you like to see?

Willingness to Change

7. Would your group be willing to make changes in the way you do business to accomplish the change needed?

8. Could you give some examples of changes you would be willing to make?

9. Would you make these changes even if you were likely to experience a period of difficulty or were uncomfortable for a period of time?

10. Would these changes be temporary or permanent?

11. Do you think other stakeholders would be willing to make changes even if the changes were difficult and would make them uncomfortable at first?

Faith in Leadership

12. Do you think the current leadership has the ability to successfully accomplish the proposed change? Why or why not?

Change Plan

13. Do you think the plan that has been described has the potential to achieve the goal(s)? Why or why not?

14. What do you think are the strong points of the plan? The weaknesses?

15. What would you change in the plan to improve it?

Skills Necessary to Implement

16. Do you think your group has the knowledge/skills necessary to implement the change plan?

17. If not, do you think your group would be willing to acquire the necessary knowledge/skills?

18. How long do you think that would take?

19. Do you think there are some members of your group who, even if willing, would be unable to acquire the necessary knowledge/skills?

Change Readiness Continuum

After gathering information concerning each stakeholder group's readiness to change, place each group's rating on the continuum for each domain, using the Change Readiness Continuum Rubric on page 160 as a guide.

Stakeholder Group

History

Ready				Intermediate				Not Ready	
10	9	8	7	6	5	4	3	2	1

Need for Change

Ready				Intermediate				Not Ready	
10	9	8	7	6	5	4	3	2	1

Willingness to Change

Ready				Intermediate				Not Ready	
10	9	8	7	6	5	4	3	2	1

Faith in Leadership

Ready				Intermediate				Not Ready	
10	9	8	7	6	5	4	3	2	1

Change Plan

Ready				Intermediate				Not Ready	
10	9	8	7	6	5	4	3	2	1

Skills Necessary to Implement

Ready				Intermediate				Not Ready	
10	9	8	7	6	5	4	3	2	1

Change Readiness Continuum Rubric

Domain	Ready	Intermediate	Not Ready
History	Views previous changes as positive and generally successful.	Has no experience with previous change. Views previous change as having insignificant effect on group.	Views previous change as generally unsuccessful. Has negative experience.
Need for Change	Recognizes that present conditions are unacceptable and that change is required at this time if progress is to be made.	Realizes that things could be better but is not completely dissatisfied with things as they are.	Does not view present condition as so negative or troublesome that this change is required. May see need for others to change but not self.
Willingness to Change	Is willing to make difficult choices (personal and group) to bring about change. Is willing to accept that change will be difficult, possibly with a long period of discomfort.	Will change if the change does not require a significant inconvenience to group.	Sees no need to change. Is resistant to doing anything significantly different that may create discomfort for group.
Faith in Leadership	Believes that the current leaders have the ability to accomplish the change.	Has no strong opinions toward leadership either positive or negative due to past experience or lack of knowledge.	Is negative toward current leaders' capabilities and/or motives in general. Doesn't believe leaders can accomplish the change.
Change Plan	Has a good understanding of the vision for the future associated with change plan. Believes that the change plan, as presented, has the potential to achieve the goal(s).	Does not have a clear understanding of the vision for the future associated with the change plan. Has doubts about major components of the change plan as the right approach to achieve the goal(s).	Does not agree with the vision of the future after the change. Does not believe the change plan, as presented, is necessary or has the potential to achieve the goal(s).
Skills Necessary to Implement	Believes the group represented has the knowledge and/or skills necessary to implement the plan.	Believes the group has some of the knowledge and/or skills necessary to implement the plan and believes that many of those who do not will be able to acquire the knowledge and/or skills.	Has serious doubts that the group represented has the knowledge and/or skills necessary to successfully implement the plan and doubts that most members of the group can acquire the knowledge and/or skills.

Stakeholder Change Readiness Matrix

Transfer the ratings from the Continuum to the Matrix, which will provide a graphic display of each group's rating on each domain.

Stakeholder Group	Domain					
	History	Need for Change	Willingness to Change	Faith in Leadership	Change Plan	Skills Necessary to Implement
Governing Body						
Local Political Governance						
Superintendent						
Senior District Leadership						
Building Administration						
Teachers						
Administrative/Teacher Organizations						
Parents						
Students						
Business Leaders						
Other Stakeholders:						

Appendix B: Freeport School District Plan on a Page, 2007–2008

VISION	GOALS AND MEASURES	ACTION PLANS
STUDENT PERFORMANCE Every student is performing at or above grade level, engaged in his or her learning, and contributing positively to the community.	• By 2010, all students in grades 3–8 will meet or exceed the ILS as measured by ISAT; by June 2008, 87% of the students will meet or exceed the Reading ILS and 92% will meet or exceed the Math ILS on ISAT. • By June 2014, all students in grade 11 will meet or exceed the ILS as measured by PSAE; by June 2008, 78% students will meet or exceed the Reading ILS and 63% students will meet or exceed the Math ILS. • For each of the next 4 years, FSD will move at least 10% of students from "meets" to "exceeds" on the State exams. By June 2010, all grade 8 students will successfully complete Algebra I or a higher level math course. By June 2008, 80% of grade 7 students will be prepared to successfully complete Algebra I or a higher level math course during the 2008–2009 school year. • By June 2010, close the achievement gap in grades 3–8, with a greater %age of all groups in the "meets" and "exceeds" categories each year. By June 2008, 81% of African American students in grades 3–8 will meet or exceed reading ILS and 85% "meet" or "exceed" math ILS. • By June 2014, close the achievement gap for grades 9–12. By June 2008, 63% of African American high school students will meet or exceed reading and math ILS. • By Sept. 2010, enrollment in high academic courses will mirror the District's ethnic make-up, while low income student group will increase annually 5%age points.	■ By Aug. 31, 2007, each school will identify students, below grade level on State exams and/or local assessments, to receive additional support to move students to grade level. ■ By June 2007, administration will review and improve its process for academic acceleration in student learning, using data/feedback/strategies process, at the District, building, and student levels. The data will be reviewed on a monthly basis, using Literacy First reading assessments (K–6), local reading assessments (K–12), and local math assessment (K–12) to develop student level strategies for improvement in both reading and math. This process will be implemented at the start of the 2007–2008 school year.
EQUITY Every person is treated fairly, promoting dignity and mutual respect. The diverse talents of all staff and students are fully appreciated and developed.	• By June 2008, African American representation in extra-curricular activities will meet MOU compliance ranges at elementary through high school, and 70% of FJHS and FHS African American students will participate in at least one extra-curricular or "school connecting" activity. • By June 2010, provide a positive learning environment as measured by 100% of staff indicating that they believe schools are safe/secure and atmosphere is conducive for learning. By June 2008, decrease suspensions and conduct referrals by 10%.	• Communicate "it's okay to be smart" message through AVID, Efficacy, student groups, parent meetings, mentoring, etc. • Enroll all grade 6 students who meet/exceed math standards or pass the Orleans math test in Pre-algebra or Algebra I. • Provide staff development in area of cultural diversity. • Counselors and other stakeholders aggressively recruit minorities and low income students for higher level courses. • Aggressively recruit minorities for extra-curricular activities and develop recruitment plans for activities with limited to no diversity. • Continue faithful implementation of Second Step. • Implement PBIS and ICLE Intervention Pyramid as part of the FHS Freshman Plan.

VISION	GOALS AND MEASURES	ACTION PLANS
PARTNERSHIPS Student, family and community partnerships contribute to the success of every student.	**Student Partnerships** • By June 2008, every student will have a set of personal academic goals that are regularly reviewed and updated at least 4 times/year by students, teachers and parents. • By June 2008, there will be an increase of 10% of students reporting a safe/caring school environment as measured by survey data. **Parent-Family Partnerships** • By June 2010, 90% of District families will have participated in a research-based parent partnership program focused on student success; by June 2008, at least 10% of District families will have participated in a research-based parent partnership program. • By June 2010, at least 90% of parents will express satisfaction with FSD 145 as measured by a District survey. **Community Partnerships:** • By June 2008, every school will have at least two community partnerships that demonstrate a positive contribution to the physical, social, emotional, and academic growth of students. **Overall:** • By June 2008, increase public awareness of FSD 145 performance beyond 2007 levels. • By June 2010, at least 90% of a valid community sample will be satisfied with FSD 145.	• Implement a plan at each school to set personal student goals by September 1, 2007. • Establish and maintain a student-focus group at each school to "listen to" and "learn from" students. • Implement programs to recognize student success. • Establish and implement an approach to engage each family in the review and support of their student's goals and plan. • Implement research-based programs to increase parent participation in support of student success. • Implement strategies to gather input from parents regarding their level of satisfaction. • Support each school's efforts to establish effective community partnerships to serve students. • Work with community partners to recruit, train and sustain an increased number of student mentors. • Establish and implement a comprehensive strategy to enhance school district communications. • Survey a cross-section of community members regarding satisfaction with district programs and services.
HUMAN RESOURCES Our diverse faculty and staff enthusiastically implement best practices and are recognized and valued for our results.	• By August 2010, teaching staff demographics will mirror the Illinois teaching demographics as identified by the State Report Card. • By 2010, the level of African American administrators in the District will have been maintained or increased. • By June 2010, 100% of staff will indicate that they are recognized and valued for district results in student performance, as measured by the annual staff survey. • By June 2010, at least 90% of a valid staff sample will indicate they are satisfied with their work.	• Modify Retention and Recruitment Plan to aggressively increase the number of African American teachers and keep a motivated and highly qualified staff. • Support "Educators for Tomorrow" by providing incentives and encouragement for students, staff, and community members to pursue careers in education. • Evaluate, modify, and aggressively improve the impact of the Staff Recognition Program. • Each school and support service department will analyze its staff survey results and develop conclusions, recommendations, and changes to accelerate improvement. • Provide quality staff development activities for all staff.

Source: Freeport School District, Freeport, IL. Copyright © 2007 by the Freeport School District. Reprinted with permission.

References

Ainsworth, L. (2003). *Power standards: Identifying the standards that matter the most.* Englewood, CO: Advanced Learning Press.

Ainsworth, L., & Viegut, D. (2006). *Common formative assessments: How to connect standards-based instruction and assessment.* Thousand Oaks, CA: Corwin Press.

Allington, R. (2005, February). Ideology is still trumping evidence. *Phi Delta Kappan,* 86(6), 462–468.

An economic case for high school reform (Editorial). (2007, November 1). *Minneapolis Star Tribune.* Available: www.startribune.com/opinion/editorials/11148976.html

Barth, R. S. (1990). *Improving schools from within: Teachers, parents, and principals can make the difference.* San Francisco: Jossey-Bass.

Beck, M. (2006). *The four-day win: How to end your diet war and achieve thinner peace four days at a time.* New York: Simon & Schuster.

Boyatzis, R. E., & McKee, A. (2005). *Resonant leadership: Renewing yourself and connecting with others through mindfulness, hope, and compassion.* Boston: Harvard Business School Press.

Buckingham, M. (2007). *Go put your strengths to work: 6 powerful steps to achieve outstanding performance.* New York: Free Press.

Burns, D. D. (1999). *The feeling good handbook.* New York: Plume.

Calkins, L. M. (1994). *The art of teaching writing* (2nd ed.). Portsmouth, NH: Heinemann.

Calkins, L. M. (2001). *The art of teaching reading.* New York: Addison-Wesley Longman.

Cappella, E., & Weinstein, R. S. (2001, December). *Journal of Educational Psychology*, *93*(4), 758–771.

Carlson, R. L., Imwinkelried, E. J., & Kionka , E. J. (1991). *Evidence in the nineties: Cases, materials, and problems for an age of science and statutes* (3rd ed.). Charlottesville, VA: Michie Company Law Publishers.

Carroll, L. (1898). *Alice's adventures in Wonderland*. New York: Macmillan.

Carter, S. (1999). *No excuses: Seven principals of low-income schools who set the standard for high achievement*. Washington, DC: Heritage Foundation.

Casciaro, T., & Lobo, M. S. (2005, June). Competent jerks, lovable fools, and the formation of social networks. *Harvard Business Review*, *83*(6), 92–99.

Cervone, L., & Martinez-Miller, P. (2007, Summer). Classroom walkthroughs as a catalyst for school improvement: Classroom walkthroughs enable teachers to get to the heart of what students are doing and understanding in a different and holistic way. *Leadership Compass*, *4*(4). Available: www.naesp.org/resources/2/Leadership_Compass/2007/LC2007v4n4a2.pdf

Chenoweth, K. (2007). *It's being done: Academic success in unexpected schools*. Boston: Harvard Education Press.

Christensen, C., Marx, M., & Stevenson, H. H. (2006, October). The tools of cooperation and change. *Harvard Business Review*, *84*(10), 72–80.

Cook, W. J. (2004). When the smoke clears. *Phi Delta Kappan*, *86*(1), 73–75.

Darling-Hammond, L., & Sykes, G. (Eds.). (1999). *Teaching as the learning profession: Handbook of policy and practice*. San Francisco: Jossey-Bass.

Davis, S., Darling-Hammond, L., LaPointe, M., & Meyerson, D. (2005). *School leadership study: Developing successful principals*. Stanford, CA: Stanford University, Stanford Educational Leadership Institute.

Deutschman, A. (2007). *Change or die: The three keys to change at work and in life*. New York: HarperCollins Publishers.

Diamond, J. M. (1999). *Guns, germs, and steel: The fates of human societies*. New York: W. W. Norton & Company.

Downey, C. J., Steffy, B. E., English, F. W., Frase, L. E., & Poston, W. K. (2004). *The three-minute classroom walk-through: Changing school supervisory practice one teacher at a time*. Thousand Oaks, CA: Corwin Press.

Edmonds, R. (1979, September). Effective schools for the urban poor. *Educational Leadership*, *37*(1), 15–24.

Elmore, R. (2009). Institutions, improvement, and practice. In A. Hargreaves & M. Fullan (Eds.), *Change wars*. Bloomington, IN: Solution Tree.

Fullan, M. (2007). *The new meaning of educational change*. New York: Teachers College Press.

Fullan, M. (2008).*The six secrets of change: What the best leaders do to help their organizations survive and thrive*. San Francisco: Jossey-Bass.

Gardner, H. (1995). *Leading minds: An anatomy of leadership*. New York: BasicBooks.

Goldberg, M. F. (2000, September). Leadership for change: An interview with John Goodlad. *Phi Delta Kappan, 82*(1), 82–85.

Goldsmith, M., & Lyons, L. S. (2006). *Coaching for leadership: The practice of leadership coaching from the world's greatest coaches* (2nd ed.). San Francisco: Pfeiffer.

Goleman, D., Boyatzis, R., & McKee, A. (2002). *Primal leadership: Realizing the power of emotional intelligence*. Boston: Harvard Business School Press.

Goodlad, J. I. (1994). *Educational renewal: Better teachers, better schools*. San Francisco: Jossey-Bass.

Guskey, T. R. (2000, December). Grading policies that work against standards . . . and how to fix them. *NASSP Bulletin, 84*(620), 20–29.

Guskey, T. R. (2002). *How's my kid doing? A parent's guide to grades, marks, and report cards*. San Francisco: Jossey Bass.

Guskey, T. R., & Bailey, J. M. (2001). *Developing grading and reporting systems for student learning*. Thousand Oaks, CA: Corwin Press.

Hargreaves, A., & Fink, D. (2006). *Sustainable leadership*. San Francisco: Jossey-Bass.

Hargreaves, A., & Fullan, M. (Eds.). (2009). *Change wars*. Bloomington, IN: Solution Tree.

Haycock, K. (1998, Summer). Good teaching matters . . . a lot. *Education Trust, 3*(2), 3–14.

Haycock, K. (1999). *Dispelling the myth: High-poverty schools exceeding expectations*. Washington, DC: Education Trust.

Heifetz, R., & Linsky, M. (2002). *Leadership on the line: Staying alive through the dangers of leading*. Boston: Harvard Business School Press.

Johnson, R. C. (2000). As studies stress link to scores, districts get tough on attendance. *Education Week, 20*(7), 1, 10.

Kennedy, R. (2006, July 27). The arts may aid literacy, study says. *New York Times*, p. E1.

Kidder, T. (2004). *Mountains beyond mountains: The quest of Dr. Paul Farmer, a man who would cure the world*. New York: Random House.

King, S. (2002). *On writing: A memoir of the craft*. New York: Pocket Books.

Kotter, J. P. (2006). *Leading change*. Boston: Harvard Business School Press.

Kotter, J. P. (2007, January). Leading change: Why transformation efforts fail. *Harvard Business Review, 85*(1), 96–103.

Kotter, J. P., & Rathgeber, H. (1995). *Our iceberg is melting: Changing and succeeding under any conditions*. Boston: Harvard Business School Press.

Kübler-Ross, E. (1969). *On death and dying: What the dying have to teach doctors, teachers, nurses, and their own family members*. New York: Touchstone.

The Leadership and Learning Center. (2008). *Innovation and remediation*. Executive summary: A collaborative project between the State of Nevada Department of Education and The Leadership and Learning Center. Englewood, CO: Author.

Leithwood, K., Louis, K., Anderson, S., & Wahlstrom, K. (2004, September). *How leadership influences student learning*. Report commissioned by the Wallace Foundation. Retrieved March 26, 2006, from www.wallacefoundation.org/KnowledgeCenter/KnowledgeTopics/EducationLeadership/HowLeadership InfluencesStudentLearning.htm

Levine, M. (2002). *The myth of laziness*. New York: Simon and Schuster.

Levitt, S. D., & Dubner, S. J. (2006). *Freakanomics: A rogue economist explores the hidden side of everything*. New York: HarperCollins Publishers.

Luecke, R. (2004). *Coaching and mentoring: How to develop top talent and achieve stronger performance*. Boston: Harvard Business School Press.

Lyon, R., & Chhabra, V. (2004, March). The science of reading research. *Educational Leadership, 61*(6), 12–17.

Marshall, K. (2006, September/October). The why's and how's of teacher evaluation rubrics. *Edge, 2*(1), 1–19.

Marzano, R. J. (2000). *Transforming classroom grading*. Alexandria, VA: ASCD.

Marzano, R. J. (2007). *The art and science of teaching: A comprehensive framework for effective instruction*. Alexandria, VA: ASCD.

Marzano, R. J., Kendall, J. S., & Cicchinelli, L. F. (1999). *What Americans believe students should know: A survey of U.S. adults*. Aurora, CO: Mid-continent Regional Educational Laboratory. Retrieved February 1, 2006, from www.mcrel.org/PDF/Standards/5987RR_WhatAmerBelieve.pdf

Marzano, R. J., Pickering, D., & Pollock, J. E. (2001). *Classroom instruction that works: Research-based strategies for increasing student achievement*. Alexandria, VA: ASCD.

Marzano, R. J., Waters, T., & McNulty, B. A. (2005). *School leadership that works: From research to results*. Alexandria, VA: ASCD.

McKee, A., Boyatzis, R., & Johnston, F. (2008). *Becoming a resonant leader: Develop your emotional intelligence, renew your relationships, sustain your effectiveness*. Boston: Harvard Business School Publishers.

Merriam-Webster's collegiate dictionary (10th ed.). (1998). Springfield, MA: Merriam-Webster.

Mitchell, R. (1996). *Front-end alignment: Using standards to steer education change—A manual for developing standards*. Washington, DC: Education Trust.

Ness, M. (2007, November). Reading comprehension strategies in secondary content-area classrooms. *Phi Delta Kappan, 89*(3), 229–231.

O'Connor, K. (2007). *A repair kit for grading: 15 fixes for broken grades*. Portland, OR: Educational Testing Service.

Peters, T. (2003). *Re-imagine! Business excellence in a disruptive age*. London: Dorling Kindersley Limited.

Peters, T. J., & Waterman, R. H., Jr. (1982). *In search of excellence: Lessons from America's best-run companies*. New York: Warner Books.

Petersen, J. L. (2007, Winter). Learning facts: The brave new world of data-informed instruction. *Education Next, 7*(1), 36–42.

Pfeffer, J., & Sutton, R. I. (2000). *The knowing-doing gap: How smart companies turn knowledge into action*. Boston: Harvard Business School Press.

Popham, W. J. (2006, November). Phony formative assessments: Buyer beware! *Educational Leadership, 64*(3), 86–87.

Porter, M. (1980). *Competitive strategy*. New York: Free Press.

Reeves, D. B. (2002). *The daily disciplines of leadership: How to improve student achievement, staff motivation, and personal organization*. San Francisco: Jossey-Bass.

Reeves, D. B. (2004a). *Accountability for learning: How teachers and school leaders can take charge*. Alexandria, VA: ASCD.

Reeves, D. B. (2004b). *Accountability in action: A blueprint for learning organizations* (2nd ed.). Englewood, CO: Advanced Learning Press.

Reeves, D. B. (2004c). *Assessing educational leaders: Evaluating performance for improved individual and organizational results*. Thousand Oaks, CA: Corwin Press.

Reeves, D. B. (2004d). The case against zero. *Phi Delta Kappan*, 86(4), 324–325.

Reeves, D. B. (2006a). Leading to change: Preventing 1,000 failures. *Educational Leadership*, 64(3), 88–89.

Reeves, D. B. (2006b). *The learning leader: How to focus school improvement for better results*. Alexandria, VA: ASCD.

Reeves, D. B. (2008). *Reframing teacher leadership to improve your school*. Alexandria, VA: ASCD.

Reeves, D. (2009). Level-five networks: Making significant change in complex organizations. In A. Hargreaves & M. Fullan (Eds.), *Change wars*. Bloomington, IN: Solution Tree.

Reeves, D. B., & Allison, E. (2009). *Renewal coaching*. San Francisco: Jossey-Bass.

Reigeluth, C. M. (2006). The guidance system for transforming education. *TechTrends*, 50(2), 42.

Rosenthal, R., & Jacobson, L. (1968). *Pygmalion in the classroom: Teacher expectation and pupils' intellectual development*. Carmarthen, Wales, UK: Crown House.

Rothstein, R. (2004). Class and the classroom: Even the best schools can't close the race achievement gap. *American School Board Journal*, 191(10), 16.

Schmoker, M. J. (2001, October 24). The Crayola curriculum. *Education Week*, 21(8), 42–44.

Schmoker, M. J. (2004). Tipping point: From feckless reform to substantive instructional improvement. *Phi Delta Kappan*, 85(6), 424–432.

Schmoker, M. (2006). *Results now: How we can achieve unprecedented improvements in teaching and learning*. Alexandria, VA: ASCD.

Senge, P., Kleiner, A., Roberts, C., Roth, G., Ross, R., & Smith, B. (1999). *The dance of change*. New York: Doubleday.

Sherman, S., & Freas, A. (2004, November). The Wild West of executive coaching. *Harvard Business Review*, 82–90.

Squire, K. D., & Reigeluth, C. M. (2000). The many faces of systemic change. *Educational Horizons*, 78(3), 143–152.

Stiggins, R. J. (2004). *Student-involved assessment for learning* (4th ed.). Upper Saddle River, NJ: Prentice-Hall.

Wagner, T., Kegan, R., Lahey, L. L., & Lemons, R. W. (2006). *Change leadership: A practical guide to transforming our schools*. San Francisco: Jossey-Bass.

Wheatley, M. J., & Frieze, D. (2007, April). Beyond networking: How large-scale change really happens. *The School Administrator*, 4(64). Retrieved May 20, 2008, from www.aasa.org/publications/saarticledetail.cfm?ItemNumber=8648&snItem Number=950&tnItemNumber=

White, S. (2005). *Beyond the numbers: Making data work for teachers and school leaders.* Englewood, CO: Advanced Learning Press.

White, S. (2009). *Leadership maps.* Englewood, CO: Lead + Learn Press.

Yun, J. T., & Moreno, J. F. (2006, January/February). College access, K–12 concentrated disadvantage, and the next 25 years of education research. *Educational Researcher, 35*(1), 12–19.

Index

Information in figures is denoted by *f*.

About the Author

Douglas B. Reeves is the founder of The Leadership and Learning Center. He has worked with education, business, nonprofit, and government organizations throughout the world. The author of more than 20 books and many articles on leadership and organizational effectiveness, he has twice been named to the Harvard University Distinguished Authors Series.

His monthly column on change leadership appears in *Educational Leadership*. Dr. Reeves was named the Brock International Laureate for his contributions to education. He also received the Distinguished Service Award from the National Association of Secondary School Principals and the Parents Choice Award for his writing for children and parents.

Related ASCD Resources: Change Leadership

At the time of publication, the following ASCD resources were available (ASCD stock numbers appear in parentheses). For up-to-date information about ASCD resources, go to www.ascd.org.

Multimedia

Creating the Capacity for Change: An ASCD Action Tool by Jody Mason Westbrook and Valarie Spisder-Albert (#702118)

Guiding School Improvement with Action Research Books-in-Action Package (10 Books and 1 video) (#700261)

Making School Improvement Happen with What Works in Schools: An ASCD Action Tool Set (Three Tools) by John L. Brown (#705055)

Schooling by Design: An ASCD Action Tool (#707039)

Networks

Visit the ASCD Web site (www.ascd.org) and click on About ASCD. Go to the section on Networks for information about professional educators who have formed groups around topics such as "Restructuring Schools." Look in the Network Directory for current facilitators' addresses and phone numbers.

Online Courses

Visit the ASCD Web site (www.ascd.org) for the following professional development opportunities:

Contemporary School Leadership by Vera Blake (#PD04OC38)

Creating and Sustaining Professional Learning Communities by Vera Blake and Diane Jackson (#PD04OC43)

What Works in Schools: An Introduction by John Brown (#PD04OC36)

Print Products

Accountability for Learning: How Teachers and School Leaders Can Take Charge by Douglas B. Reeves (#104004)

Align the Design: A Blueprint for School Improvement by Nancy J. Mooney and Ann T. Mausbach (#108005)

Connecting Leadership with Learning: A Framework for Reflection, Planning, and Action by Michael Copland and Michael Knapp (#105003)

Educational Leadership, February 2005: How Schools Improve (#105032)

Educational Leadership, May 2006: Challenging the Status Quo (#106043)

Enhancing Student Achievement: A Framework for School Improvement by Charlotte Danielson (#102109)

How to Help Your School Thrive Without Breaking the Bank by John G. Gabriel and Paul C. Farmer (#107042)

Leadership Capacity for Lasting School Improvement by Linda Lambert (#102283)

Leadership for Learning: How to Help Teachers Succeed by Carl D. Glickman (#101031)

The Learning Leader: How to Focus School Improvement for Better Results by Douglas B. Reeves (#105151)

The Results Fieldbook: Practical Strategies from Dramatically Improved Schools by Mike Schmoker (#101001)

Results Now: How We Can Achieve Unprecedented Improvements in Teaching and Learning by Mike Schmoker (#106045)

Transforming Schools: Creating a Culture of Continuous Improvement by Allison Zmuda, Robert Kuklis, and Everett Kline (#103112)

Video and DVD

What Works in Schools (DVD and Facilitator's Guide) (#603047)

Leadership Strategies for Principals (DVD and *The New Principal's Fieldbook: Strategies for Success* by Pam Robbins and Harvey Alvy) (#608033)

The Results Video Series (DVD and Online Facilitator's Guide) (#601261)

A Visit to a Data-Driven School District (DVD and Viewer's Guide) (#606059)

THE WHOLE CHILD The Whole Child Initiative helps schools and communities create learning environments that allow students to be healthy, safe, engaged, supported, and challenged. To learn more about other books and resources that relate to the whole child, visit www.wholechildeducation.org.

For more information, visit us on the World Wide Web (http://www.ascd.org); send an e-mail message to member@ascd.org; call the ASCD Service Center (1-800-933-ASCD or 703-578-9600, then press 2); send a fax to 703-575-5400; or write to Information Services, ASCD, 1703 N. Beauregard St., Alexandria, VA 22311-1714 USA.